PROPERTY OF

_____
(Notary Public's legal signature)

IF FOUND, please immediately contact:

Notary's Printed Name: _____

Notary's Email: _____

Notary's Business Address: _____

Notary's Telephone: _____
     (cell)   *(work)*   *(home)*

COMMISSION & JOURNAL INFORMATION

My _____ notary public commission (# _____) runs from _____ to _____
 (state of jurisdiction e.g. CA)   *(commencement)*   *(expiration)*

Bond: _____ _____ _____
  (issuing company)   *(address)*   *(phone)*   *(bond number)*

Errors & Omissions Insurance: _____ (policy # _____) runs from _____ to _____
     (issuing company)   *(commencement)*   *(expiration)*

This journal _____ records official notarial acts from _____ to _____ and entry # _____ to _____
  (number)   *(start date)*   *(end date)*

DEATH/INCAPACITY and PRESERVATION INSTRUCTIONS

In the event of the death or incapacity of the above-named notary public, this journal must be mailed to:

_____

_____ within _____

Pursuant to state law, this notary journal shall be preserved for at least _____ years from its final entry or the commi

i

To Stacey~

My eternal gratitude for his abiding love, support and encouragement to pursue my dreams

(including the creation of this book)

... and for making my heart smile every single day.

NOTARY JOURNAL FOR GEORGIA: A Notary Public's Comprehensive Quick-Fill 100-Entry Log Book / Register of Official Notarial Acts & Records

ISBN No. 978-1-69-888498-1
First paperback printing 2019
Published by Notary Records, LLC

LEGAL DISCLAIMER: NEITHER THE AUTHOR NOR THE PUBLISHER ASSUMES ANY RESPONSIBILITY OR LIABILITY WHATSOEVER ON BEHALF OF THE CONSUMER OR READER OF THE MATERIAL IN THIS BOOK. THE INFORMATION PROVIDED IN THIS BOOK DOES NOT, AND IS NOT INTENDED TO, CONSTITUTE LEGAL ADVICE, IS INSTEAD PROVIDED ONLY FOR GENERAL INFORMATIONAL PURPOSES, AND SHOULD NOT BE USED TO REPLACE THE SPECIALIZED TRAINING AND PROFESSIONAL JUDGMENT OF A LICENSED/COMMISSIONED NOTARY PUBLIC OR COMPETENT ATTORNEY. NEITHER THE AUTHOR NOR THE PUBLISHER CAN BE HELD RESPONSIBLE OR LIABLE FOR THE USE OF THE INFORMATION PROVIDED VIA THIS BOOK.

Created by a Woman-Owned Business

and

★★★ Proudly Printed in the UNITED STATES OF AMERICA ★★★

NOTARY JOURNAL for GEORGIA

A NOTARY PUBLIC'S
COMPREHENSIVE QUICK-FILL 100-ENTRY LOG BOOK /
REGISTER OF OFFICIAL NOTARIAL ACTS & RECORDS

BY
JENNA JACK

iii

AUTHOR's NOTE

Notaries serve as our nation's first line of defense against identity theft and other types of fraud by protecting the PUBLIC (their clients) and the integrity of our LEGAL SYSTEM during signings ... **but NOTARIES deserve protection too.** Although just one third of U.S. states require it, many others strongly encourage use of a record book, and increasingly more advocate recording more data[1] than their state law requires (e.g. "any other information the notary considers appropriate" C.R.S. 12-55-111(3)(f)). Choosing a comprehensive <u>notary journal</u> is one invaluable way we notaries can protect ourselves.

After several years as a California notary public, I found myself still searching for a really efficient notary journal with a more <u>spacious</u> and <u>logical</u> layout that had data-dedicated areas to capture <u>ALL</u> of the legally required information for many common notarial acts. However, the more time I spent searching for my ideal notary journal, the more I realized that it did not exist ... yet.

My goal for this book was to create the most **COMPREHENSIVE** yet **EFFICIENT, SPACIOUS, WELL-ORGANIZED, QUICK-FILL, SINGLE-PAGE entry** in a truly **MULTI-STATE** notary journal ... but also make it budget-friendly by offering it at a much **LOWER PRICE-PER-ENTRY** than many.

This book is the culmination of two years of research, planning, testing and care. It began with thorough analysis of notary journal layouts from more than 50 publishers, which inspired me to create nearly 80 quick-fill options (pre-printed prompts to circle and checkboxes to mark) to minimize the data a notary must write out longhand. **Check just one box** to indicate: [1] any of seven 7 types of notarial acts [2] the signer's representative capacity [3] the notary's personal knowledge (or lack thereof) of a credible witness [4] administration of an oath or affirmation to a credible witness [5] a signer's signature by mark[6] an inspection or copy request or [7] an incomplete notarial service.

Investigation of various state laws governing journals and notarial acts in the United States was my next step. While there is much overlap among the applicable laws of the 50 states, <u>many small but significant legal distinctions exist as to what each U.S. state requires to lawfully complete any given notarial act.</u> This multi-state notary journal endeavors to accommodate the laws of 49 U.S. states (excepting Hawaii which requires a smaller book size) so that each notary can take the precautions she or he deems appropriate to minimize her or his liability.

Determining how to combine the substantive journal entry requirements of each U.S. state in a smart yet spacious format was my final and biggest challenge -- the fingerprint and all signature blocks for signer and credible witnesses are easily accessible at the paper's right-hand edge (not at the book binding) and marked with easy locator symbols, yet all related data are still conveniently grouped together. The landscape orientation provides larger spaces for bigger writing and enables the journal entry to fit on a single page [2 entries per page] (that means no more writing into or across a book binding gutter to complete an entry).

I appreciate being able to look at a completed journal entry and quickly confirm from the data-dedicated areas and pre-printed prompts that I have recorded all of the appropriate information for the given circumstances. I hope you find that this multi-state notary journal helps you notarize more efficiently and effectively.

Jenna Jack

1 – Record additional data as long as it does not otherwise violate state law (e.g. do not record fingerprints if your state prohibits doing so).

ELEMENTS of JOURNAL ENTRY

Notaries protect the PUBLIC (their clients) and the LEGAL SYSTEM from identity theft and other fraud . . . **but NOTARIES deserve protection too.** Aside from continuing study, the most valuable tool we notaries have to protect ourselves from liability is the NOTARY JOURNAL we select. Beyond recording the facts of the notarized document or proceeding, each journal entry is an *official business record* . . . and a *good journal entry* thoroughly evidences the protocol followed by the notary (to the notary's protection).

Increasingly more states encourage their notaries to record more data than their state law requires (e.g. "any other information the notary considers appropriate" C.R.S. 12-55-111(3)(f)). This **MULTI-STATE** journal strikes a unique balance in being **EFFICIENT** and **LOGICAL** *but also* **COMPREHENSIVE.**

Each entry has **nearly 80 quick-fill[a] options** (over 45 checkboxes to mark and over 30 items to circle) throughout **data-dedicated spaces** for orderly recording all of the below elements. But in addition to the traditional notarization data, this **cutting-edge journal** equips the notary to quickly capture the below-starred elements (★) newly required by one or more U.S. states in the 4 intuitive left-edge tabs of its spacious half-page entry:

NOTARIZATION SERVICE	DOCUMENT/PROCEEDING	SIGNER	CREDIBLE WITNESS(ES)
date of notarization	doc/proceeding **type** [box]	**personal knowledge** [box] *or*	**printed names** of both credible witnesses
★ **time** of notarization	doc/proceeding **date**	**satisfactory evidence** [box] via	★ **personally known** to notary [box]
★ **address** of notarization	doc/proceeding **title**	**identification** [box] *or*	★ **addresses** of both credible witnesses
★ notary's **office** [box]	★ number of **pages** to doc	**credible witness** [box]	★ address **non-disclosure** [box]
notarization **act type** [box]	★ **inspect/copy** request [box]	signer's **printed name**	credible witness **phone numbers** [circle]
notes	★ entry **cross-reference #**	★ signer's **representative capacity** [box]	credible witness **IDs types** [box]
★ **mileage**		signer's **address**	**serial #s** of credible witness IDs
notary **service fee**		★ address **non-disclosure** [box]	**agency** issuing credible witness IDs
★ related **clerical fees** [box]		signer's **phone number** [circle]	**issue dates** of credible witness IDs *and*
(travel, rush, copy, other)		signer's **ID type** [box]	**expiration dates** of credible witness IDs
★ **incomplete** service [box]		**serial #** of signer's ID	★ **oaths** given to both credible witnesses [box]
★ **notary name**		**agency** issuing signer's ID	★ **oath** indicators [circle]
★ notary **commission #**		**issue date** of signer's ID *and*	★ **affirmation** indicators [circle]
journal **entry #**		**expiration date** of signer's ID	**signatures** of both credible witnesses
journal **page #**		★ any **oath** given to signer [box]	**miscellaneous** information [box]
		★ **oath** indicator [circle]	
		★ **affirmation** indicator [circle]	
		signature of signer	
		★ signature **by mark** [box]	
		fingerprint of signer	
		★ **hand** indicator [circle]	
		★ **finger** indicator [circle]	
		miscellaneous information [box]	

[a] **Quick-Fill options**

[box] indicates a checkbox to tick

[circle] indicates an item to circle

THIS CONTENT IS COPYRIGHTED © 2019 Jenna Jack

ATTRIBUTES of JOURNAL ENTRY
(entry is actual size relative to page)

pre-printed page numbers

sequential pre-printed journal entry numbers

large outside-edge fingerprint box with convenient horizontal imprint orientation and finger identification (right/left hand and thumb/index/middle/ring/pinky fingers)

entry cross-reference area

inspection/copy checkbox

note special circumstances (e.g. signer's capacity/physical condition/willingness; fee details like waiting time, travel start & stop time; check "Stop" and indicate reason for any unfulfilled notarization; describe "other" notarization acts)

track all state-permitted fees and record *advance* client consent by checking boxes

4 distinct logical sections to capture all details of
1. notary service
2. underlying document
3. signer and
4. credible witness #1 & #2

nearly 80 quick-fill checkboxes & items to circle to save time & enhance accuracy

easy locator symbols for signer (arrow) and witnesses (#1 & #2) with checkboxes for oath/affirmation and signature by mark' in large outside-edge signature boxes

signer's entity capacity checkbox (e.g. V.P. of X corporation)

note public inspection prohibition for battered signer/witness address

3 miscellaneous catch-all checkboxes for extra or uncommon information

dedicated space for printed name and address of signer and BOTH credible witnesses

credible witness personally known to notary checkboxes

Journal Entry (entry form)

796

Fingerprint

R (T) I M R P (L)

Page 398

TOTAL FEES
□ Other $64.64

□ Stop MILES 8 Notary $15 Adv. Travel $24.64 $.25 □ Rush $0 □ Copy $0.64

□ Office NOTES CareMore Convalescent

Entry X-Ref # 836

SERVICE
DATE 06-29-2019 TIME 10:30 (am) pm
TYPE □ Acknowledgment ☒ Jurat □ Oath/Affirmation □ Copy Certification □ Signature Witnessing □ Oath of Office □ Protest □ Other

DOCUMENT
DOC TYPE □ Deed G/QC/W □ DOT/Mortgage □ Trust Rev/Irrev/Cert □ Will □ POAF G/L D/S □ POAH/AHCD ☒ Affidavit □ Other
DOC DATE J F M A M (J) J A S O N D 29, 2019
DOC TITLE or TYPE Affidavit of Death of Trustee
OF PAGES 1 □ Inspect □ Copy Request

ADDRESS 789 Post St. SF 94111

SIGNER
☒ SATISFACTORY EVIDENCE □ Driver's License / Passport / Other ID OR ☒ Credible Witness(es) or □ Personal Knowledge
SIGNER's NAME Jane M. Smith
SIGNATURE Jane M. Smith ☒ (oath/affirmation, if any) □ (by Mark)
□ Driver's License □ Passport ☒ Non-Public # □ Other ID □ ISSUED □ EXPIRES AGENCY
ADDRESS 123 Main Street #4 San Francisco, CA 94104 □ For
PHONE C / H / W
burn/victim (fingerprint) □ P/Known ☒ MISC.

CW #1
#1 WITNESS's NAME Mary A. Jones
SIGNATURE Mary A. Jones ☒ (after oath/affirmation) ①
☒ Driver's License □ Passport □ Non-Public # C1234123 □ Other ID ISSUED 2/14/17 EXPIRES 2/14/22 AGENCY CA DMV
ADDRESS 123 Main Street #6 San Francisco, CA 94104
PHONE (C) H / W 415/555-1234 □ P/Known □ MISC.

CW #2
#2 WITNESS's NAME Roberta C. Adams
SIGNATURE Roberta C. Adams ☒ (after oath/affirmation) ②
□ Driver's License ☒ Passport □ Non-Public # 123456789 □ Other ID ISSUED 7/4/16 EXPIRES 7/4/26 AGENCY U.S. Dept. of State
ADDRESS 135 Main Street San Francisco, CA 94104
PHONE C / H / (W) 415/555-1515 □ P/Known □ MISC.

vii

OATH & AFFIRMATION SCRIPTS

(suggestion: attach a printed copy of the verbiage for oaths and affirmations that you administer to signers, credible witnesses and others)

DUTY OF CONFIDENTIALITY

Regardless of the state in which you are commissioned, **safeguarding the confidentiality of the client data recorded in your notary journal is one of the most fundamental and paramount of a notary public's duties.** The American Association of Notaries directs notaries to "cover any previous journal entries" when meeting with a client. That means concealing ALL prior entries from the current client, credible witness(es) and anyone else present during EACH of your notarizations.

Fines, criminal charges, and suspension or even revocation of a notary's commission are among the disciplinary sanctions that many states impose for failure to follow applicable notarial laws. Because many states have enacted umbrella legislation (e.g. "failure to discharge fully and faithfully any of the duties or responsibilities required of a notary public" Cal. Gov. Code § 8214.1(d)), the violation of which is subject to discipline, preserving the confidentiality of your clients' data is a serious matter not to be taken lightly.

Fortunately, **concealing all prior journal entries from your next client is now easy** … due to the innovative half-page entry format of this landscape orientation notary journal (it opens upwards like a calendar). Regardless of which of the 4 entries you use (top entry on upper page, bottom entry on upper page, top entry on lower page, or bottom entry on lower page), my companion Data Shield effortlessly conceals all visible prior entries recorded in any of the Jenna Jack notary journals.

Email me to learn more or to order your budget-friendly custom-designed bi-fold **DATA SHIELD**.

Thank you,

Jenna Jack

NotaryRecords@gmail.com

NOTES

(suggestion: record notes or place post-it here noting things to follow up on)

VARIANCES in U.S. STATE LAWS seamlessly accommodated by this MULTI-STATE JOURNAL

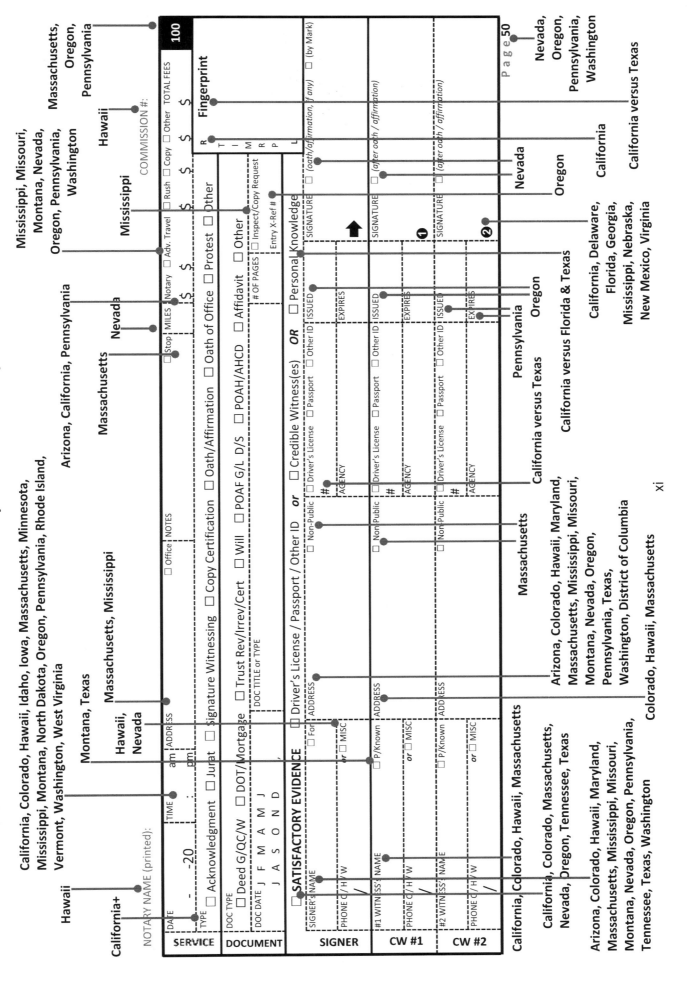

Massachusetts, Oregon, Pennsylvania

Hawaii

Mississippi, Missouri, Montana, Nevada, Oregon, Pennsylvania, Washington

Mississippi

Arizona, California, Pennsylvania

Nevada

Massachusetts

Massachusetts, Mississippi

Hawaii, Nevada

Montana, Texas

Hawaii

California+

California, Colorado, Hawaii, Idaho, Iowa, Massachusetts, Minnesota, Mississippi, Montana, North Dakota, Oregon, Pennsylvania, Rhode Island, Vermont, Washington, West Virginia

Nevada, Oregon, Pennsylvania, Washington

California versus Texas

California

Oregon

Nevada

California, Delaware, Florida, Georgia, Mississippi, Nebraska, New Mexico, Virginia

Oregon

Pennsylvania

California versus Texas

California versus Florida & Texas

Massachusetts

Arizona, Colorado, Hawaii, Maryland, Massachusetts, Mississippi, Missouri, Montana, Nevada, Oregon, Pennsylvania, Texas, Washington, District of Columbia

California, Colorado, Hawaii, Massachusetts

California, Colorado, Massachusetts, Nevada, Oregon, Tennessee, Texas

Arizona, Colorado, Hawaii, Maryland, Massachusetts, Mississippi, Missouri, Montana, Nevada, Oregon, Pennsylvania, Tennessee, Texas, Washington

Colorado, Hawaii, Massachusetts

xi

THIS MULTI-STATE NOTARY JOURNAL ACCOMMODATES:

★ THE LAWS OF 49 U.S. STATES[1]

including SELECT LAWS UNIQUE to the following 27 STATES[2] (see pages xiii – xvii):

Arizona	Nebraska
California	Nevada
Colorado	New Mexico
Delaware	North Dakota
Florida	Oregon
Georgia	Pennsylvania
Idaho	Rhode Island
Iowa	Tennessee
Maryland	Texas
Massachusetts	Vermont
Minnesota	Virginia
Mississippi	Washington and
Missouri	West Virginia as well as
Montana	the District of Columbia and

★ THE REVISED UNIFORM LAW ON NOTARIAL ACTS (RULONA)

NOTE: *The design and content of this multi-state notary journal is based on research current through July 2019.*

[1] except Hawaii which requires a smaller book size.

[2] that mandate use of a record book and/or that have adopted RULONA.

STATE-SPECIFIC* LAWS ACCOMMODATED by this MULTI-STATE NOTARY JOURNAL © 2019 Jenna Jack

[NOTARIZATION] SERVICE TAB

1 TIME - - California, Colorado, Hawaii, Idaho, Iowa, Massachusetts, Minnesota, Mississippi, Montana, North Dakota, Oregon, Pennsylvania, Rhode Island, Vermont, Washington and West Virginia require recording of the time of notarization in the notary journal.

2 SERVICE ADDRESS - - Massachusetts and Mississippi require recording of the address where the notarization occurs. Simply check the "Office" box if the notarization is performed onsite at the notary's office.

3 NOTES - - Record any special circumstances in the "NOTES" box (e.g. the signer's capacity/physical condition/willingness, waiting time, extra fee details or as Nevada requires the notary's start and stop travel times). If any notarization goes unfulfilled, check the "Stop" box and note the reason as Massachusetts requires.

4 FEES - - Many states including Mississippi, Missouri, Montana, Nevada, Oregon, Pennsylvania and Washington require the notary service fee to be separately itemized in the notary journal from any clerical or administrative costs (e.g. mileage reimbursement, travel time, rush charge, waiting time, cancellation and copy costs). Each notary should research his or her own state's particular laws which may require (1) advance disclosure of all clerical/administrative costs as separate and unregulated from any notary service fee and (2) the client's advance agreement to pay them. Check the various fee boxes to evidence your advance disclosure of any clerical/administrative costs (however Pennsylvania requires clerical fees on the client's receipt rather than in the notary journal). If no fee is charged for the notarial service, many states require recording of that fact such as Arizona (enter ∅), California (enter $0) or Pennsylvania (enter N/C or $0).

5 SERVICE TYPE - - Most states require recording of the type of notarial service act (e.g. jurat, acknowledgment). However, California advises against using abbreviations or acronyms and instead strongly encourages recording the whole word(s) in the notary journal. Check one box to record the appropriate unabbreviated service type.

797

SERVICE								

DATE - -20 **TIME** : □ am ● **1** □ pm **ADDRESS** □ Office **2** NOTES □ **3** Stop MILES Notary □ Adv. Travel □ Rush □ Copy □ Other **TOTAL FEES 4**
$ $ $ $ $ $

TYPE 5 □ Acknowledgment □ Jurat □ Signature Witnessing □ Copy Certification □ Oath/Affirmation □ Oath of Office □ Protest □ Other

DOC TYPE □ Deed G/QC/W □ DOT/Mortgage □ Trust Rev/Irrev/Cert □ Will □ POAF G/L D/S □ POAH/AHCD □ Affidavit □ Other

DOC DATE - J F M A M J J A S O N D , **6** **DOC TITLE or TYPE** # OF PAGES **7** □ Inspect/Copy Request Entry X-Ref # **8**

Fingerprint 9
R
T
I
M
R
P
L

□ **SATISFACTORY EVIDENCE** □ Driver's License / Passport / Other ID **or** □ Credible Witness(es) **OR** □ Personal Knowledge

SIGNER's NAME 10 □ For **11** ADDRESS □ Non-Public **13** □ Driver's License □ Passport □ Other ID **14** ISSUED **14** Other ID # **14** SIGNATURE □ (oath/affirmation, if any) □ (by Mark) **15**
PHONE C / H / W or □ MISC **12** AGENCY **14** EXPIRES

#1 WITNESS's NAME **16** P/Known ADDRESS **17** □ Non-Public □ Driver's License □ Passport □ Other ID **14** ISSUED **14** Other ID # SIGNATURE □ (after oath / affirmation) **18** ❶
PHONE C / H / W or □ MISC **12** AGENCY **14** EXPIRES

#2 WITNESS's NAME **16** P/Known ADDRESS **17** □ Non-Public □ Driver's License □ Passport □ Other ID **14** ISSUED **14** Other ID # SIGNATURE □ (after oath / affirmation) **19** ❷
PHONE C / H / W or □ MISC **12** AGENCY **14** EXPIRES

DOCUMENT	SIGNER	CW #1	CW #2

---

* The information provided herein does not, and is not intended to, constitute legal advice and instead is provided only for general informational purposes. References to specific notary laws of the 50 U.S. states serve only as illustration and are not exhaustive. Because all such references are current only through July 2019, **EACH NOTARY IS SOLELY RESPONSIBLE FOR RESEARCHING AND KEEPING ABREAST OF THE NOTARY LAWS APPLICABLE IN THE PARTICULAR STATE IN WHICH SHE OR HE IS COMMISSIONED.**

STATE-SPECIFIC* LAWS ACCOMMODATED by this MULTI-STATE NOTARY JOURNAL © 2019 Jenna Jack

DOCUMENT TAB

❻ DOCUMENT DATE -- **Colorado, Hawaii, Montana** and **Texas** require recording of the date of the document being notarized. Because multiple dates are often recorded for any given notarization, this journal's unique date format (notary hand writes the numeric day and year but circles the 1st letter of the appropriate month) helps to call attention to this critical date to ensure the correct document date is legibly recorded.

❼ DOCUMENT LENGTH -- It is good notarial practice to record the number of pages to any document being notarized (to discourage fraudulent document or page swapping) so be sure to count accurately. **Hawaii** requires recording the number of pages of the notarized document in the *notarial certificate*.

❽ INSPECTION/COPY REQUEST -- **Mississippi** and the Revised Uniform Law On Notarial Acts ("RULONA" adopted by **Colorado, Idaho, Iowa, Minnesota, Montana, North Dakota, Oregon, Pennsylvania, Rhode Island, Vermont, Washington** and **West Virginia**) require any request to inspect or copy a notary journal entry to be recorded as a separate distinct entry in the notary's journal. Mark the checkbox, circle "Inspect" or "Copy" in both the original and current journal entries and write the original journal entry number as a cross-reference in the inspection/copy request journal entry after "Entry X-Ref #".

❾ FINGERPRINT -- Many states require recording of the signer's <u>right thumbprint</u> for notarization of certain documents (e.g. powers of attorney and most documents affecting real estate in **California**) so circle "R" for right hand and "T" for thumb. **California** notaries must designate if an alternate finger is used so simply circle the corresponding letter to denote the thumb, index, middle, ring or pinky finger and "L" if the left hand is used. <u>Do not</u> fingerprint clients in states like **Texas** that prohibit doing so due to their strict regulations regarding collection and retention of biometric data.

797

DATE	TIME ① am / pm	☐ Stop MILES ☐ Notary ☐ Adv. Travel ☐ Rush ☐ Copy ☐ Other TOTAL FEES ④

| ADDRESS ② | ☐ Office NOTES ③ | Fingerprint ⑨ R T I M R P L |

SERVICE — TYPE ⑤ ☐ Acknowledgment ☐ Jurat ☐ Signature Witnessing ☐ Copy Certification ☐ Oath/Affirmation ☐ Oath of Office ☐ Protest ☐ Other

DOCUMENT — DOC TYPE ☐ Deed G/QC/W ☐ DOT/Mortgage ☐ Trust Rev/Irrev/Cert ☐ Will ☐ POAF G/L D/S ☐ POAH/AHCD ☐ Affidavit ☐ Other

DOC DATE ⑥ J F M A M J J A S O N D , DOC TITLE or TYPE

OF PAGES ⑦ ☐ Inspect/Copy Request ⑧ Entry X-Ref

SIGNER ⑩ SATISFACTORY EVIDENCE ☐ Driver's License / Passport / Other ID **or** ☐ Credible Witness(es) **OR** ☐ Personal Knowledge

SIGNER's NAME ⑪ ☐ For ☐ Non-Public ☐ Driver's License ☐ Passport ☐ Other ID ⑬ Other ID ISSUED ⑭ EXPIRES ⑭ SIGNATURE ☐ (oath/affirmation, if any) ☐ (by Mark) ⑮

PHONE C / H / W or ☐ MISC ⑫ # ⑯ ADDRESS ⑰ AGENCY

CW #1 #1 WITNESS's NAME ☐ P/Known ☐ Non-Public ☐ Driver's License ☐ Passport ☐ Other ID Other ID ISSUED ⑭ EXPIRES ⑭ SIGNATURE ☐ (after oath/affirmation) ⑱ ❶

PHONE C / H / W or ☐ MISC ⑫ # ⑯ ADDRESS ⑰ AGENCY

CW #2 #2 WITNESS's NAME ☐ P/Known ☐ Non-Public ☐ Driver's License ☐ Passport ☐ Other ID Other ID ISSUED ⑭ EXPIRES ⑭ SIGNATURE ☐ (after oath/affirmation) ⑲ ❷

PHONE C / H / W or ☐ MISC ⑫ # ⑯ ADDRESS ⑰ AGENCY

STATE-SPECIFIC* LAWS ACCOMMODATED by this MULTI-STATE NOTARY JOURNAL © 2019 Jenna Jack

SIGNER TAB

🔟 **SATISFACTORY EVIDENCE** -- Many U.S. states like **California, Colorado, Massachusetts, Nevada, Oregon, Tennessee** and **Texas** require recording whether the notary identified the signer through (1) personal knowledge or (2) satisfactory evidence, being (a) proper identification or (b) a credible witness(es). Some states including **California** no longer allow identification of the signer through personal knowledge. Be sure to mark the two applicable checkboxes for Satisfactory Evidence cases.

⓫ **SIGNER'S NAME** -- **Arizona, Colorado, Hawaii, Maryland, Massachusetts, Mississippi, Missouri, Montana, Nevada, Oregon, Pennsylvania, Tennessee, Texas** and **Washington** require recording the signer's printed name. While **California** does not, it is good notarial practice to do so because signatures are often illegible. For those signing in a representative capacity (e.g. President or Vice-President of a corporation), check the "For" box and an empty "MISC" box (in the Credible Witness tab) and record the signer's work title (capacity) and employer/entity name beside it, or alternatively in the NOTES area (in the Service tab.)

⓬ **MISCELLANEOUS** -- Check the "MISC" box and record any extra information required by your state if the phone number of the signer or credible witness(es) is not required (e.g. **Hawaii** requires recording of the names of other parties to the instrument; **Nevada** requires the notary's travel start and stop times).

⓭ **SIGNER'S ADDRESS** -- Although **Pennsylvania** requires only the city and state, **Arizona, Colorado**, the **District of Columbia, Hawaii, Maryland, Massachusetts, Mississippi, Missouri, Montana, Oregon, Texas** and **Washington** require recording the signer's full address. Although **California** requires neither, pinpointing the signer's identity is good notarial practice (and better protects the notary). Use the convenient checkbox for states like **Massachusetts** that require notation in the journal that a battered signer's address is not subject to public inspection.

⓮ **IDENTIFICATION DATES** -- While **Oregon** requires recording of only the date of issuance of identification presented by a signer or witness, **Pennsylvania** requires recording of both the date of issuance AND the date of expiration for any identification presented by a signer or any witness.

⓯ **SIGNER'S SIGNATURE** -- A large black arrow differentiates the signer's signature box that is conveniently located on the right outside edge of the journal for the client's comfort. Use the checkbox to indicate a 'signature by mark' or as **Nevada** requires any oath or affirmation taken by the signer and circle which one was administered.

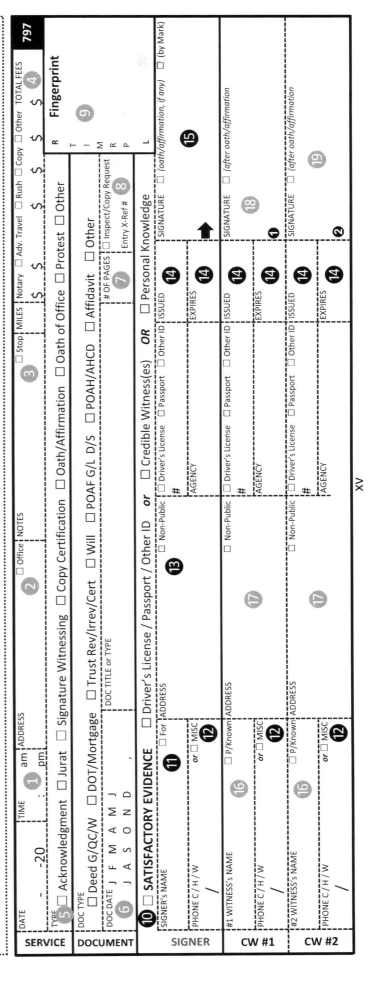

STATE-SPECIFIC* LAWS ACCOMMODATED by this MULTI-STATE NOTARY JOURNAL © 2019 Jenna Jack

CREDIBLE WITNESS TAB

16 CREDIBLE WITNESS NAME -- **California, Colorado, Hawaii** and **Massachusetts** require recording of the printed name of any witnesses to the notarization. Many states like **California** permit a single credible witness to serve as satisfactory evidence of the identity of a signer who does not possess (and it would be difficult/impossible to obtain) proper identification IF the witness personally knows the signer and is personally known by the notary. **Montana** and **Texas** permit a single credible witness not personally know by the notary IF proper identification is presented. Indicate the notary's personal knowledge (or lack thereof) of the credible witness via the "P/Known" checkbox.

17 CREDIBLE WITNESS ADDRESS -- **Colorado, Hawaii** and **Massachusetts** require recording of the address of any witnesses to the notarization. Use the convenient checkbox for states like **Massachusetts** that require notation in the journal that a battered witness's address is not subject to public inspection.

18 CREDIBLE WITNESS #1 SIGNATURE -- A black-circled #1 differentiates the signature box for the 1st credible witness that is conveniently located on the journal's *right outside edge*. As **Nevada** requires, affirmatively evidence the oath/affirmation given to the 1st credible witness by marking the checkbox and circling which one was given.

19 CREDIBLE WITNESS #2 SIGNATURE -- **California, Delaware, Florida, Georgia, Mississippi, Nebraska, New Mexico** and **Virginia** permit two credible witnesses (who are not personally known by the notary) to serve as satisfactory evidence of the identity of the signer (who does not possess proper identification) IF both credible witnesses personally know the signer *and* present proper identification. A black-circled #2 differentiates the signature box for the 2nd credible witness that is conveniently located on the journal's *right outside edge* for their comfort. Use the checkbox to affirmatively evidence the oath/affirmation given to the 2nd credible witness and circle which one was given. **Pennsylvania** requires recording of the credible witness data (name, address, ID) in the *same journal entry* as the underlying notarization being conducted on the signer's behalf. For states like **Oregon** that require recording of the credible witness data in a *separate journal entry* from the signer's underlying notarization, enter the two corresponding journal entry cross-reference numbers in the respective "Entry X-ref #" spaces (in the Inspect/Copy Request area) of both journal entries.

797

SERVICE
- DATE ___ - ___ -20___   TIME ___ : ___ ☐ am ☐ pm
- ☐ Stop ☐ MILES ☐ Notary ☐ Adv. Travel ☐ Rush ☐ Copy ☐ Other TOTAL FEES
  $ ___ $ ___ $ ___ $ ___ $ ___ $ ___
- ☐ Office   NOTES

DOCUMENT
- TYPE: ☐ Acknowledgment ☐ Jurat ☐ Signature Witnessing ☐ Copy Certification ☐ Oath/Affirmation ☐ Oath of Office ☐ Protest ☐ Other
- DOC TYPE: ☐ Deed G/QC/W ☐ DOT/Mortgage ☐ Trust Rev/Irrev/Cert ☐ Will ☐ POAF G/L D/S ☐ POAH/AHCD ☐ Affidavit ☐ Other
- DOC DATE ___ / J F M A M J J A S O N D , ___   DOC TITLE or TYPE
- # OF PAGES ___ ☐ Inspect/Copy Request Entry X-Ref # ___

Fingerprint
R T I M R P L

SIGNER
- ☐ SATISFACTORY EVIDENCE ☐ Driver's License / Passport / Other ID *or* ☐ Credible Witness(es) *OR* ☐ Personal Knowledge
- SIGNER's NAME ___ ☐ For ☐ P/Known ☐ Non-Public
- PHONE C / H / W ___ / ___ *or* ☐ MISC
- ☐ Driver's License ☐ Passport ☐ Other ID ADDRESS
- SIGNATURE ___ ☐ (oath/affirmation, if any) ☐ (by Mark)

CW #1
- #1 WITNESS's NAME ___ ☐ P/Known ☐ Non-Public
- PHONE C / H / W ___ / ___ *or* ☐ MISC
- ☐ Driver's License ☐ Passport ☐ Other ID ADDRESS
- ISSUED ___ # ___
- EXPIRES ___ AGENCY ___
- SIGNATURE ___ ☐ (after oath/affirmation)

CW #2
- #2 WITNESS's NAME ___ ☐ P/Known ☐ Non-Public
- PHONE C / H / W ___ / ___ *or* ☐ MISC
- ☐ Driver's License ☐ Passport ☐ Other ID ADDRESS
- ISSUED ___ # ___
- EXPIRES ___ AGENCY ___
- SIGNATURE ___ ☐ (after oath/affirmation)

STATE-SPECIFIC* LAWS ACCOMMODATED by this MULTI-STATE NOTARY JOURNAL © 2019 Jenna Jack

JOURNAL FORMAT & MAINTENANCE

20 NOTARY's INFORMATION -- **Hawaii** requires the notary to legibly print her or his name and commission number respectively at the top left and top right of the page for any journal entry.

21 SEQUENTIAL ENTRY NUMBERS -- Many states like **Montana, Oregon** and **Pennsylvania** require a permanently bound journal with pre-printed sequential numbered journal entries.

22 SEQUENTIAL PAGE NUMBERS -- Many states like **Nevada, Oregon, Pennsylvania** and **Washington** require notary journal pages to be sequentially numbered.

23 JOURNAL SIZE -- The size and (calendar) landscape orientation of this softbound notary journal accommodate the requirements of 49 U.S. states (except Hawaii due to book size). Some journals claim to accommodate the laws of all 50 U.S. states when they do not. For example, Hawaii requires a *softbound* book no more than 11 inches high and no more than 16.5 inches wide *when open* (which very few journals are). Other journals lack page or journal entry numbers so do your homework when shopping.

24 JOURNAL ABBREVIATIONS -- Many states like **Oregon** require the abbreviations used by the notary to be listed in a Legend or Glossary in the journal (see page xiii).

25 JOURNAL RETENTION -- Many states like **Arizona** (5 years), **Massachusetts** (7 years), **Montana** (10 years), **Nevada** (7 years), **Oregon** (10 years), **Washington** (10 years) and **states adopting RULONA** (10 years) require notary journals to be retained for specified periods after the final entry is complete or the notary's commission ends. This requirement is addressed in the notary's information page (see page i).

26 JOURNAL SURRENDER -- In the event of a notary's death or other circumstances where she or he is no longer commissioned, many states like **Arizona, California, Colorado, Hawaii, Mississippi, Montana** (optional for resignation/termination), **Oregon, Pennsylvania, Texas**, states adopting **RULONA** and the **District of Columbia** require surrender of the notary journal (some to the Secretary of State, County Clerk/Recorder, Office of the Attorney General, state archives or other specified agency/entity). This requirement is addressed in the notary's information page (see page i).

---

20 NOTARY NAME (printed): _____ COMMISSION #: _____ **20** **21** 797

DATE ___-___-20___	TIME ___:___ ☐ am ☐ pm **1**	ADDRESS ☐ Office NOTES

SERVICE
TYPE **5** ☐ Acknowledgment ☐ Jurat ☐ Signature Witnessing ☐ Copy Certification ☐ Oath/Affirmation ☐ Protest ☐ Stop ☐ Adv. Travel ☐ Rush ☐ Copy ☐ Other TOTAL FEES
MILES ☐ Notary ☒ Oath of Office ☐ Other **3** **2** **4**

DOCUMENT
DOC TYPE ☐ Deed G/QC/W ☐ DOT/Mortgage ☐ Trust Rev/Irrev/Cert ☐ Will ☐ POAF G/L D/S ☐ POAH/AHCD ☐ Affidavit ☐ Other
6 DOC DATE ___-___ J F M A M J J A S O N D DOC TITLE or TYPE _____ # OF PAGES ☐ Inspect/Copy Request Entry-X-Ref # **8** **7**

Fingerprint
R
T
I **9**
M
R
P
L

SIGNER
10 ☐ SATISFACTORY EVIDENCE ☐ Driver's License / Passport / Other ID *or* ☐ Credible Witness(es) *OR* ☐ Personal Knowledge
SIGNER's NAME **11** ☐ For ☐ Non-Public ☐ Driver's License ☐ Passport ☐ Other ID ISSUED **14** EXPIRES **14** SIGNATURE **15** ☐ (oath/affirmation, if any) ☐ (by Mark)
PHONE C / H / W ___/___ **16** *or* ☐ MISC **12** ADDRESS **13** # _____ AGENCY _____ ⬆

CW #1
#1 WITNESS's NAME **17** ☐ P/Known ☐ Driver's License ☐ Passport ☐ Other ID ISSUED **14** EXPIRES **14** SIGNATURE **18** ☐ (after oath / affirmation)
PHONE C / H / W ___/___ **16** *or* ☐ MISC **12** ADDRESS # _____ AGENCY _____ ❶

CW #2
#2 WITNESS's NAME **17** ☐ P/Known ☐ Driver's License ☐ Passport ☐ Other ID ISSUED **14** EXPIRES **14** SIGNATURE **19** ☐ (after oath / affirmation)
PHONE C / H / W ___/___ **12** ADDRESS # _____ AGENCY _____ ❷

ILLUSTRATIONS

for

JOURNAL ENTRY USAGE OPTIONS

ENTRY ILLUSTRATION A © Jenna Jack

SERVICE	DATE 06-29-2019	TIME 9:05 (am) pm	□ Office NOTES □ Stop MILES 16	Notary ⊠ $15	Adv. Travel $9.28	Rush ⊠ $10	Copy □ $0	Other □ $0	TOTAL FEES $34.28	**798**

Fingerprint

R / T — I M R P L

ADDRESS 111 Broadway #1 SF 94111 AAA Title Company

TYPE: ⊠ Acknowledgment □ Jurat □ Signature Witnessing □ Copy Certification □ Oath/Affirmation □ Oath of Office □ Protest □ Other

DOCUMENT

DOC TYPE: ⊠ Deed □ G/QC/W □ DOT/Mortgage □ Trust Rev/Irrev/Cert □ Will □ POAF G/L D/S □ POAH/AHCD □ Affidavit □ Other

DOC TITLE or TYPE Grant Deed

DOC DATE: J F M A M (J) J A S O N D 28, 2019

OF PAGES 2   □ Inspect/Copy Request Entry X-Ref

SIGNER

SATISFACTORY EVIDENCE ⊠ Driver's License / Passport / Other ID *or* □ Credible Witness(es) **OR** □ Personal Knowledge

⊠ For □ Non-Public ⊠ Driver's License □ Passport □ Other ID ISSUED 12/25/18

ADDRESS 123 Main Street #4 # C1234567 EXPIRES 12/25/23

San Francisco, CA 94104 AGENCY CA DMV

SIGNATURE (oath/affirmation, if any) John L. Smith ↑ □ (by Mark)

SIGNER's NAME John L. Smith

PHONE C / (H) / W 415/555-1111

CW #1

□ P/Known or □ MISC □ Non-Public □ Driver's License □ Passport □ Other ID ISSUED

ADDRESS # EXPIRES AGENCY

SIGNATURE (after oath/affirmation) ❶

#1 WITNESS's NAME

PHONE C / H / W

CW #2

□ P/Known or ⊠ MISC □ Non-Public □ Driver's License □ Passport □ Other ID ISSUED

ADDRESS # EXPIRES AGENCY

SIGNATURE (after oath/affirmation) ❷

#2 WITNESS's NAME

PHONE C / H / W V.P. / ABC Corporation – Real Estate Division

NOTE: The above illustration is an introduction on *how a notary public can efficiently use the format of this notary journal entry*. It is provided for general informational purposes only and is not to be used as an example of how to correctly perform notarization services for an acknowledgment, or any other notarial act, in any given U.S. state. This illustration does not, and is not intended to, constitute legal advice. Each notary public is solely responsible for researching and keeping abreast of the notary laws currently applicable in the particular state in which she or he is commissioned.

THIS CONTENT IS COPYRIGHTED

ENTRY ILLUSTRATION B © Jenna Jack

SERVICE	DATE 06-29-2019 TIME 10:30 (am)/pm	☐ Office ☐ Stop MILES 8	Notary $15	☐ Adv. Travel ☒ Rush ☐ Copy ☐ Other TOTAL FEES
	ADDRESS 789 Post St., SF 94111 NOTES CareMore Convalescent		$24.64 $25 $0 $0 $64.64	

	Fingerprint
R (T) I M R P (L)	

TYPE ☐ Acknowledgment ☒ Jurat ☐ Signature Witnessing ☐ Copy Certification ☐ Oath/Affirmation ☐ Oath of Office ☐ Protest ☐ Other

DOCUMENT

DOC TYPE ☐ Deed G/QC/W ☐ DOT/Mortgage ☐ Trust Rev/Irrev/Cert ☐ Will ☐ POAF G/L D/S ☐ POAF G/L D/S ☐ POAH/AHCD ☒ Affidavit ☐ Other

DOC DATE J F M A M (J) J A S O N D 29, 2019   # OF PAGES 1   ☒ Inspect/Copy/Request Entry X-Ref # 836

DOC TITLE or TYPE Affidavit of Death of Trustee

☒ SATISFACTORY EVIDENCE ☐ Driver's License / Passport / Other ID **or** ☒ Credible Witness(es) **OR** ☐ Personal Knowledge

	SIGNER'S NAME Jane M. Smith ☐ For ☒ MISC	☒ Non-Public ☐ Driver's License ☐ Passport ☐ Other ID #	ISSUED	SIGNATURE ☒ (oath)/affirmation, if any) ☐ (by Mark) *Jane M. Smith*
SIGNER	ADDRESS 123 Main Street #4 San Francisco, CA 94104	AGENCY	EXPIRES	⬆
	PHONE C / H / W burn/Victim (fingerprint)			

	#1 WITNESS's NAME Mary A. Jones ☐ P/Known **or** ☐ MISC	☐ Non-Public ☒ Driver's License ☐ Passport ☐ Other ID # C1234123	ISSUED 2/14/17	SIGNATURE ☒ (after oath/affirmation) *Mary A. Jones*
CW #1	ADDRESS 123 Main Street #6 San Francisco, CA 94104	AGENCY CA DMV	EXPIRES 2/14/22	❶
	PHONE (C)/ H / W 415/555-1234			

	#2 WITNESS's NAME Roberta C. Adams ☐ P/Known **or** ☐ MISC	☐ Non-Public ☐ Driver's License ☒ Passport ☐ Other ID # 123456789	ISSUED 7/4/16	SIGNATURE ☒ (after oath/affirmation) *Roberta C. Adams*
CW #2	ADDRESS 135 Main Street San Francisco, CA 94104	AGENCY U.S. Dept. of State	EXPIRES 7/4/26	❷
	PHONE C / H /(W) 415/555-1515			

799

NOTE: The above illustration is an introduction on *how a notary public can efficiently use the format of this notary journal entry.* It is provided for general informational purposes only and is not to be used as an example of how to correctly perform notarization services for a jurat, or any other notarial act, in any given U.S. state. This illustration does not, and is not intended to, constitute legal advice. Each notary public is solely responsible for researching and keeping abreast of the notary laws currently applicable in the particular state in which she or he is commissioned.

ENTRY ILLUSTRATION C © Jenna Jack

SERVICE	DATE 06-29-2019	TIME 11:45 (am) pm	☑ Office ☐ Stop	NOTES Stroke immobile (signature)

800

☐ Stop | MILES | Notary ☐ Adv. Travel ☑ Rush ☐ Copy ☐ Other | TOTAL FEES
0 | $15 $0 | $10 $0 | $0 | $25.00

Fingerprint

(R)T — I M R P L

DOCUMENT

TYPE
☑ Acknowledgment ☐ Jurat ☐ Signature Witnessing ☐ Copy Certification ☐ Oath/Affirmation ☐ Oath of Office ☐ Protest ☐ Other

DOC TYPE
☐ Deed G/QC/W ☐ DOT/Mortgage ☐ Trust Rev/Irrev/Cert ☐ Will ☐ POAF G/L D/S ☐ POAF/AHCD ☐ Affidavit ☑ Other

DOC DATE J F M A M (J) J A S O N D 27, 2019 — DOC TITLE or TYPE: Assignment of Property to Cho Revocable Trust

OF PAGES 1 | ☑ Inspect ☑ Copy Request | Entry X-Ref # 842

SIGNER

☑ SATISFACTORY EVIDENCE ☑ Driver's License / Passport / Other ID *or* ☐ Credible Witness(es) *OR* ☐ Personal Knowledge

SIGNER's NAME: Christina P. Cho
PHONE (C) H / W: 415/555-5678

☑ For ☐ Non-Public | ADDRESS 111 Oak Street | San Francisco, CA 94111

☑ Driver's License ☐ Passport ☐ Other ID #C1231234 | AGENCY CA DMV | ISSUED 11/24/16 | EXPIRES 11/24/21

SIGNATURE ☐ *(oath/affirmation, if any)* ☒ *(by Mark)*

X — Christina P. Cho
by

CW #1

#1 WITNESS's NAME: Amelia E. Gutierrez
PHONE (C) H / W: 415/555-5555

☐ P/Known ☐ or ☐ MISC | ADDRESS 123 Penny Lane | San Francisco, CA 94111

☐ Driver's License ☐ Passport ☐ Other ID # | AGENCY | ISSUED | EXPIRES

SIGNATURE ☐ *(after oath/affirmation)*
❶ Amelia E. Gutierrez

CW #2

#2 WITNESS's NAME:
PHONE C / H / W:

☐ P/Known ☐ or ☐ MISC | ADDRESS | ☐ Non-Public

☐ Driver's License ☐ Passport ☐ Other ID # | AGENCY | ISSUED | EXPIRES

SIGNATURE ☐ *(after oath/affirmation)*
❷

NOTE: The above illustration is an introduction on *how a notary public can efficiently use the format of this notary journal entry.* It is provided for general informational purposes only and is <u>not</u> to be used as an example of how to correctly perform notarization services for a signature by mark, or any other notarial act, in any given U.S. state. This illustration does not, and is not intended to, constitute legal advice. Each notary public is solely responsible for researching and keeping abreast of the notary laws currently applicable in the particular state in which she or he is commissioned.

FEE SCHEDULE

(suggestion: store a laminated copy of your fee schedule including rush, after hours, waiting time, cancellation, travel, mileage, and copy costs)

LEGEND of NOTARY's ABBREVIATIONS

(suggestion: attach a printed copy of abbreviations that you build over the course of your notary career)

TO MOST EFFECTIVELY USE THIS NOTARY JOURNAL

(for example, why and how best to use the "Stop" "For" or "Non-Public" checkboxes)

see

"STATE-SPECIFIC LAWS ACCOMMODATED BY THIS MULTI-STATE NOTARY JOURNAL"

for explanations about items in the

SERVICE tab . . . . page xiii

DOCUMENT tab . . . . page xiv

SIGNER tab . . . . page xv

CREDIBLE WITNESS tab . . . . page xvi

JOURNAL FORMAT & MAINTENANCE . . . . page xvii

NOTARY NAME (printed): _____

COMMISSION #: _____

Entry 1

SERVICE											TOTAL FEES
☐ Stop	☐ MILES	Notary	☐ Adv. Travel	☐ Rush	☐ Copy	☐ Other					
		$	$	$	$	$	$	$	$		$

DATE ___ - ___ -20___ TIME ___ : ___ ☐ am ☐ pm ADDRESS _____ ☐ Office NOTES

SERVICE — TYPE: ☐ Acknowledgment ☐ Jurat ☐ Signature Witnessing ☐ Copy Certification ☐ Oath/Affirmation ☐ Protest ☐ Other

DOCUMENT — DOC TYPE: ☐ Deed G/QC/W ☐ DOT/Mortgage ☐ Trust Rev/Irrev/Cert ☐ Will ☐ POAF G/L D/S ☐ POAH/AHCD ☐ Affidavit ☐ Oath of Office ☐ Other

DOC DATE J F M A M J J A S O N D , ___ DOC TITLE or TYPE _____ # OF PAGES ___ ☐ Inspect/Copy Request ☐ Entry X-Ref #

SIGNER

☐ **SATISFACTORY EVIDENCE** — Driver's License / Passport / Other ID **or** ☐ Credible Witness(es) **OR** ☐ Personal Knowledge

SIGNER's NAME _____ ☐ For _____ ☐ Non-Public ☐ Driver's License ☐ Passport ☐ Other ID ISSUED _____ EXPIRES _____ SIGNATURE ☐ (oath/affirmation, if any) ☐ (by Mark)

PHONE C / H / W _____ / _____ **or** ☐ MISC # _____ AGENCY _____

CW #1

#1 WITNESS's NAME _____ ☐ P/Known ADDRESS _____ ☐ Non-Public ☐ Driver's License ☐ Passport ☐ Other ID ISSUED _____ EXPIRES _____ SIGNATURE ☐ (after oath / affirmation)

PHONE C / H / W _____ / _____ **or** ☐ MISC # _____ AGENCY _____ ❶

CW #2

#2 WITNESS's NAME _____ ☐ P/Known ADDRESS _____ ☐ Non-Public ☐ Driver's License ☐ Passport ☐ Other ID ISSUED _____ EXPIRES _____ SIGNATURE ☐ (after oath / affirmation)

PHONE C / H / W _____ / _____ **or** ☐ MISC # _____ AGENCY _____ ❷

Fingerprint

R
T
I
M
R
P
L

Entry 2

SERVICE											TOTAL FEES
☐ Stop	☐ MILES	Notary	☐ Adv. Travel	☐ Rush	☐ Copy	☐ Other					
		$	$	$	$	$	$	$	$		$

DATE ___ - ___ -20___ TIME ___ : ___ ☐ am ☐ pm ADDRESS _____ ☐ Office NOTES

SERVICE — TYPE: ☐ Acknowledgment ☐ Jurat ☐ Signature Witnessing ☐ Copy Certification ☐ Oath/Affirmation ☐ Protest ☐ Other

DOCUMENT — DOC TYPE: ☐ Deed G/QC/W ☐ DOT/Mortgage ☐ Trust Rev/Irrev/Cert ☐ Will ☐ POAF G/L D/S ☐ POAH/AHCD ☐ Affidavit ☐ Oath of Office ☐ Other

DOC DATE J F M A M J J A S O N D , ___ DOC TITLE or TYPE _____ # OF PAGES ___ ☐ Inspect/Copy Request ☐ Entry X-Ref #

SIGNER

☐ **SATISFACTORY EVIDENCE** — Driver's License / Passport / Other ID **or** ☐ Credible Witness(es) **OR** ☐ Personal Knowledge

SIGNER's NAME _____ ☐ For _____ ☐ Non-Public ☐ Driver's License ☐ Passport ☐ Other ID ISSUED _____ EXPIRES _____ SIGNATURE ☐ (oath/affirmation, if any) ☐ (by Mark)

PHONE C / H / W _____ / _____ **or** ☐ MISC # _____ AGENCY _____

CW #1

#1 WITNESS's NAME _____ ☐ P/Known ADDRESS _____ ☐ Non-Public ☐ Driver's License ☐ Passport ☐ Other ID ISSUED _____ EXPIRES _____ SIGNATURE ☐ (after oath / affirmation)

PHONE C / H / W _____ / _____ **or** ☐ MISC # _____ AGENCY _____ ❶

CW #2

#2 WITNESS's NAME _____ ☐ P/Known ADDRESS _____ ☐ Non-Public ☐ Driver's License ☐ Passport ☐ Other ID ISSUED _____ EXPIRES _____ SIGNATURE ☐ (after oath / affirmation)

PHONE C / H / W _____ / _____ **or** ☐ MISC # _____ AGENCY _____ ❷

Fingerprint

R
T
I
M
R
P
L

Entry 3

3 | **Fingerprint**

R
T
I M
R
P
L

SERVICE	DATE __ - __ -20__	TIME __ : __	☐ am ☐ pm	ADDRESS	☐ Office	NOTES	☐ Stop	☐ MILES	☐ Notary	☐ Adv. Travel	☐ Rush	☐ Copy	☐ Other	TOTAL FEES
								$	$	$	$	$	$	$

TYPE: ☐ Acknowledgment ☐ Jurat ☐ Signature Witnessing ☐ Copy Certification ☐ Oath/Affirmation ☐ Protest ☐ Other

DOCUMENT
DOC TYPE: ☐ Deed G/QC/W ☐ DOT/Mortgage ☐ Trust Rev/Irrev/Cert ☐ Will ☐ POAF G/L D/S ☐ POAH/AHCD ☐ Affidavit ☐ Other
DOC DATE J F M A M J J A S O N D , ____ **DOC TITLE or TYPE** ____ # OF PAGES ____ ☐ Inspect/Copy Request Entry X-Ref # ____

SIGNER
☐ **SATISFACTORY EVIDENCE** ☐ Driver's License / Passport / Other ID **or** ☐ Credible Witness(es) **OR** ☐ Personal Knowledge
SIGNER's NAME ____ ☐ For ☐ Non-Public ADDRESS ____ ☐ Driver's License ☐ Passport ☐ Other ID ISSUED ____ SIGNATURE ____ ☐ (oath/affirmation, if any) ☐ (by Mark)
PHONE C / H / W ____ / ____ **or** ☐ MISC # ____ AGENCY ____ EXPIRES ____

CW #1
#1 WITNESS's NAME ____ ☐ P/Known ☐ Non-Public ADDRESS ____ ☐ Driver's License ☐ Passport ☐ Other ID ISSUED ____ SIGNATURE ____ ☐ (after oath / affirmation) ❶
PHONE C / H / W ____ / ____ **or** ☐ MISC # ____ AGENCY ____ EXPIRES ____

CW #2
#2 WITNESS's NAME ____ ☐ P/Known ☐ Non-Public ADDRESS ____ ☐ Driver's License ☐ Passport ☐ Other ID ISSUED ____ SIGNATURE ____ ☐ (after oath / affirmation) ❷
PHONE C / H / W ____ / ____ **or** ☐ MISC # ____ AGENCY ____ EXPIRES ____

Entry 4

4 | **Fingerprint**

R
T
I M
R
P
L

SERVICE	DATE __ - __ -20__	TIME __ : __	☐ am ☐ pm	ADDRESS	☐ Office	NOTES	☐ Stop	☐ MILES	☐ Notary	☐ Adv. Travel	☐ Rush	☐ Copy	☐ Other	TOTAL FEES
								$	$	$	$	$	$	$

TYPE: ☐ Acknowledgment ☐ Jurat ☐ Signature Witnessing ☐ Copy Certification ☐ Oath/Affirmation ☐ Protest ☐ Other

DOCUMENT
DOC TYPE: ☐ Deed G/QC/W ☐ DOT/Mortgage ☐ Trust Rev/Irrev/Cert ☐ Will ☐ POAF G/L D/S ☐ POAH/AHCD ☐ Affidavit ☐ Other
DOC DATE J F M A M J J A S O N D , ____ **DOC TITLE or TYPE** ____ # OF PAGES ____ ☐ Inspect/Copy Request Entry X-Ref # ____

SIGNER
☐ **SATISFACTORY EVIDENCE** ☐ Driver's License / Passport / Other ID **or** ☐ Credible Witness(es) **OR** ☐ Personal Knowledge
SIGNER's NAME ____ ☐ For ☐ Non-Public ADDRESS ____ ☐ Driver's License ☐ Passport ☐ Other ID ISSUED ____ SIGNATURE ____ ☐ (oath/affirmation, if any) ☐ (by Mark)
PHONE C / H / W ____ / ____ **or** ☐ MISC # ____ AGENCY ____ EXPIRES ____

CW #1
#1 WITNESS's NAME ____ ☐ P/Known ☐ Non-Public ADDRESS ____ ☐ Driver's License ☐ Passport ☐ Other ID ISSUED ____ SIGNATURE ____ ☐ (after oath / affirmation) ❶
PHONE C / H / W ____ / ____ **or** ☐ MISC # ____ AGENCY ____ EXPIRES ____

CW #2
#2 WITNESS's NAME ____ ☐ P/Known ☐ Non-Public ADDRESS ____ ☐ Driver's License ☐ Passport ☐ Other ID ISSUED ____ SIGNATURE ____ ☐ (after oath / affirmation) ❷
PHONE C / H / W ____ / ____ **or** ☐ MISC # ____ AGENCY ____ EXPIRES ____

NOTARY NAME (printed): _____ COMMISSION #: _____

Entry 5

SERVICE

DATE ___ - ___ -20___ TIME ___:___ am/pm ADDRESS _____ NOTES _____

☐ Office ☐ Stop ☐ MILES ☐ Notary ☐ Adv. Travel ☐ Rush ☐ Copy ☐ Other TOTAL FEES

$ ____ $ ____ $ ____ $ ____ $ ____ $ ____

Fingerprint

R
T
I
M
R
P
L

DOCUMENT

TYPE: ☐ Acknowledgment ☐ Jurat ☐ Signature Witnessing ☐ Copy Certification ☐ Oath/Affirmation ☐ Oath of Office ☐ Protest ☐ Other

DOC TYPE: ☐ Deed G/QC/W ☐ DOT/Mortgage ☐ Trust Rev/Irrev/Cert ☐ Will ☐ POAF G/L D/S ☐ POAH/AHCD ☐ Affidavit ☐ Other

DOC DATE ___ - ___ J F M A M J J A S O N D   DOC TITLE or TYPE ____ # OF PAGES ___ ☐ Inspect/Copy Request Entry X-Ref # ___

SIGNER

SATISFACTORY EVIDENCE ☐ Driver's License / Passport / Other ID *or* ☐ Personal Knowledge *OR* ☐ Credible Witness(es)

SIGNER's NAME _____ ☐ For ☐ Non-Public ADDRESS _____ ☐ Driver's License ☐ Passport ☐ Other ID ISSUED ___ SIGNATURE ☐ (oath/affirmation, if any) ☐ (by Mark)

PHONE C / H / W ___ / ___ *or* ☐ MISC # ___ AGENCY ___ EXPIRES ___

CW #1

#1 WITNESS's NAME _____ ☐ P/Known ADDRESS _____ ☐ Driver's License ☐ Passport ☐ Other ID ISSUED ___ SIGNATURE ☐ (after oath / affirmation) ❶

PHONE C / H / W ___ / ___ *or* ☐ MISC # ___ AGENCY ___ EXPIRES ___

CW #2

#2 WITNESS's NAME _____ ☐ P/Known ADDRESS _____ ☐ Driver's License ☐ Passport ☐ Other ID ISSUED ___ SIGNATURE ☐ (after oath / affirmation) ❷

PHONE C / H / W ___ / ___ *or* ☐ MISC # ___ AGENCY ___ EXPIRES ___

Entry 6

SERVICE

DATE ___ - ___ -20___ TIME ___:___ am/pm ADDRESS _____ NOTES _____

☐ Office ☐ Stop ☐ MILES ☐ Notary ☐ Adv. Travel ☐ Rush ☐ Copy ☐ Other TOTAL FEES

$ ____ $ ____ $ ____ $ ____ $ ____ $ ____

Fingerprint

R
T
I
M
R
P
L

DOCUMENT

TYPE: ☐ Acknowledgment ☐ Jurat ☐ Signature Witnessing ☐ Copy Certification ☐ Oath/Affirmation ☐ Oath of Office ☐ Protest ☐ Other

DOC TYPE: ☐ Deed G/QC/W ☐ DOT/Mortgage ☐ Trust Rev/Irrev/Cert ☐ Will ☐ POAF G/L D/S ☐ POAH/AHCD ☐ Affidavit ☐ Other

DOC DATE ___ - ___ J F M A M J J A S O N D   DOC TITLE or TYPE ____ # OF PAGES ___ ☐ Inspect/Copy Request Entry X-Ref # ___

SIGNER

SATISFACTORY EVIDENCE ☐ Driver's License / Passport / Other ID *or* ☐ Personal Knowledge *OR* ☐ Credible Witness(es)

SIGNER's NAME _____ ☐ For ☐ Non-Public ADDRESS _____ ☐ Driver's License ☐ Passport ☐ Other ID ISSUED ___ SIGNATURE ☐ (oath/affirmation, if any) ☐ (by Mark)

PHONE C / H / W ___ / ___ *or* ☐ MISC # ___ AGENCY ___ EXPIRES ___

CW #1

#1 WITNESS's NAME _____ ☐ P/Known ADDRESS _____ ☐ Driver's License ☐ Passport ☐ Other ID ISSUED ___ SIGNATURE ☐ (after oath / affirmation) ❶

PHONE C / H / W ___ / ___ *or* ☐ MISC # ___ AGENCY ___ EXPIRES ___

CW #2

#2 WITNESS's NAME _____ ☐ P/Known ADDRESS _____ ☐ Driver's License ☐ Passport ☐ Other ID ISSUED ___ SIGNATURE ☐ (after oath / affirmation) ❷

PHONE C / H / W ___ / ___ *or* ☐ MISC # ___ AGENCY ___ EXPIRES ___

NOTARY NAME (printed): _____   COMMISSION #: _____

Entry 7

SERVICE
- DATE: __ - __ -20__   TIME: __:__ am / pm   ADDRESS _____   □ Office   NOTES _____
- □ Stop   MILES   □ Notary   □ Adv. Travel   □ Rush   □ Copy   □ Other   TOTAL FEES
  - $___ $___ $___ $___ $___ $___ $___ $___

DOCUMENT
- TYPE: □ Acknowledgment   □ Jurat   □ Signature Witnessing   □ Copy Certification   □ Oath/Affirmation   □ Oath of Office   □ Protest   □ Other
- DOC TYPE: □ Deed G/QC/W   □ DOT/Mortgage   □ Trust Rev/Irrev/Cert   □ Will   □ POAF G/L D/S   □ POAH/AHCD   □ Affidavit   □ Other
- DOC DATE: J F M A M J / J A S O N D , ___   DOC TITLE or TYPE _____
- # OF PAGES ___   □ Inspect/Copy Request   Entry X-Ref # ___

SIGNER
- **SATISFACTORY EVIDENCE** □ Driver's License / Passport / Other ID   *or*   □ Credible Witness(es)   **OR**   □ Personal Knowledge
- SIGNER's NAME _____   ADDRESS _____   □ For   □ Non-Public
- PHONE C / H / W ___ / ___   *or* □ MISC   □ Driver's License   □ Passport   □ Other ID   ISSUED ___
- # ___   AGENCY ___   EXPIRES ___   SIGNATURE ___ □ (oath/affirmation, if any)   □ (by Mark)

CW #1
- #1 WITNESS's NAME _____   ADDRESS _____   □ P/Known   □ Non-Public
- PHONE C / H / W ___ / ___   *or* □ MISC   □ Driver's License   □ Passport   □ Other ID   ISSUED ___
- # ___   AGENCY ___   EXPIRES ___   SIGNATURE ___ □ (after oath / affirmation)   ❶

CW #2
- #2 WITNESS's NAME _____   ADDRESS _____   □ P/Known   □ Non-Public
- PHONE C / H / W ___ / ___   *or* □ MISC   □ Driver's License   □ Passport   □ Other ID   ISSUED ___
- # ___   AGENCY ___   EXPIRES ___   SIGNATURE ___ □ (after oath / affirmation)   ❷

Fingerprint
- R T I M R P L

Entry 8

SERVICE
- DATE: __ - __ -20__   TIME: __:__ am / pm   ADDRESS _____   □ Office   NOTES _____
- □ Stop   MILES   □ Notary   □ Adv. Travel   □ Rush   □ Copy   □ Other   TOTAL FEES
  - $___ $___ $___ $___ $___ $___ $___ $___

DOCUMENT
- TYPE: □ Acknowledgment   □ Jurat   □ Signature Witnessing   □ Copy Certification   □ Oath/Affirmation   □ Oath of Office   □ Protest   □ Other
- DOC TYPE: □ Deed G/QC/W   □ DOT/Mortgage   □ Trust Rev/Irrev/Cert   □ Will   □ POAF G/L D/S   □ POAH/AHCD   □ Affidavit   □ Other
- DOC DATE: J F M A M J / J A S O N D , ___   DOC TITLE or TYPE _____
- # OF PAGES ___   □ Inspect/Copy Request   Entry X-Ref # ___

SIGNER
- **SATISFACTORY EVIDENCE** □ Driver's License / Passport / Other ID   *or*   □ Credible Witness(es)   **OR**   □ Personal Knowledge
- SIGNER's NAME _____   ADDRESS _____   □ For   □ Non-Public
- PHONE C / H / W ___ / ___   *or* □ MISC   □ Driver's License   □ Passport   □ Other ID   ISSUED ___
- # ___   AGENCY ___   EXPIRES ___   SIGNATURE ___ □ (oath/affirmation, if any)   □ (by Mark)

CW #1
- #1 WITNESS's NAME _____   ADDRESS _____   □ P/Known   □ Non-Public
- PHONE C / H / W ___ / ___   *or* □ MISC   □ Driver's License   □ Passport   □ Other ID   ISSUED ___
- # ___   AGENCY ___   EXPIRES ___   SIGNATURE ___ □ (after oath / affirmation)   ❶

CW #2
- #2 WITNESS's NAME _____   ADDRESS _____   □ P/Known   □ Non-Public
- PHONE C / H / W ___ / ___   *or* □ MISC   □ Driver's License   □ Passport   □ Other ID   ISSUED ___
- # ___   AGENCY ___   EXPIRES ___   SIGNATURE ___ □ (after oath / affirmation)   ❷

Fingerprint
- R T I M R P L

NOTARY NAME (printed): _____ COMMISSION #: _____

Entry 9

SERVICE		
DATE: __ - __ -20__ TIME: __ : __ am/pm	ADDRESS: _____ ☐ Office	NOTES: _____
☐ Stop ☐ MILES ☐ Notary ☐ Adv. Travel ☐ Rush ☐ Copy ☐ Other TOTAL FEES		
$ ___ $ ___ $ ___ $ ___ $ ___		

Fingerprint
R T I M R P L

TYPE: ☐ Acknowledgment ☐ Jurat ☐ Signature Witnessing ☐ Copy Certification ☐ Oath/Affirmation ☐ Oath of Office ☐ Protest ☐ Other

DOCUMENT

DOC TYPE: ☐ Deed G/QC/W ☐ DOT/Mortgage ☐ Trust Rev/Irrev/Cert ☐ Will ☐ POAF G/L D/S ☐ POAH/AHCD ☐ Affidavit ☐ Other

DOC DATE J F M A M J J A S O N D ___ / ___ , ___ DOC TITLE or TYPE: _____

OF PAGES ___ ☐ Inspect/Copy Request Entry X-Ref # ___

SIGNER

SATISFACTORY EVIDENCE ☐ Driver's License / Passport / Other ID *or* ☐ Credible Witness(es) **OR** ☐ Personal Knowledge

SIGNER's NAME: _____ ☐ Non-Public ☐ For *or* ☐ MISC

ADDRESS: _____

PHONE C / H / W: _____

☐ Driver's License ☐ Passport ☐ Other ID # ___ AGENCY ___ ISSUED ___ EXPIRES ___

SIGNATURE ☐ (oath/affirmation, if any) ☐ (by Mark) ⬆

CW #1

#1 WITNESS's NAME: _____ ☐ Non-Public ☐ P/Known *or* ☐ MISC

ADDRESS: _____

PHONE C / H / W: _____

☐ Driver's License ☐ Passport ☐ Other ID # ___ AGENCY ___ ISSUED ___ EXPIRES ___

SIGNATURE ☐ (after oath / affirmation) ❶

CW #2

#2 WITNESS's NAME: _____ ☐ Non-Public ☐ P/Known *or* ☐ MISC

ADDRESS: _____

PHONE C / H / W: _____

☐ Driver's License ☐ Passport ☐ Other ID # ___ AGENCY ___ ISSUED ___ EXPIRES ___

SIGNATURE ☐ (after oath / affirmation) ❷

Entry 10

SERVICE		
DATE: __ - __ -20__ TIME: __ : __ am/pm	ADDRESS: _____ ☐ Office	NOTES: _____
☐ Stop ☐ MILES ☐ Notary ☐ Adv. Travel ☐ Rush ☐ Copy ☐ Other TOTAL FEES		
$ ___ $ ___ $ ___ $ ___ $ ___		

Fingerprint
R T I M R P L

TYPE: ☐ Acknowledgment ☐ Jurat ☐ Signature Witnessing ☐ Copy Certification ☐ Oath/Affirmation ☐ Oath of Office ☐ Protest ☐ Other

DOCUMENT

DOC TYPE: ☐ Deed G/QC/W ☐ DOT/Mortgage ☐ Trust Rev/Irrev/Cert ☐ Will ☐ POAF G/L D/S ☐ POAH/AHCD ☐ Affidavit ☐ Other

DOC DATE J F M A M J J A S O N D ___ / ___ , ___ DOC TITLE or TYPE: _____

OF PAGES ___ ☐ Inspect/Copy Request Entry X-Ref # ___

SIGNER

SATISFACTORY EVIDENCE ☐ Driver's License / Passport / Other ID *or* ☐ Credible Witness(es) **OR** ☐ Personal Knowledge

SIGNER's NAME: _____ ☐ Non-Public ☐ For *or* ☐ MISC

ADDRESS: _____

PHONE C / H / W: _____

☐ Driver's License ☐ Passport ☐ Other ID # ___ AGENCY ___ ISSUED ___ EXPIRES ___

SIGNATURE ☐ (oath/affirmation, if any) ☐ (by Mark) ⬆

CW #1

#1 WITNESS's NAME: _____ ☐ Non-Public ☐ P/Known *or* ☐ MISC

ADDRESS: _____

PHONE C / H / W: _____

☐ Driver's License ☐ Passport ☐ Other ID # ___ AGENCY ___ ISSUED ___ EXPIRES ___

SIGNATURE ☐ (after oath / affirmation) ❶

CW #2

#2 WITNESS's NAME: _____ ☐ Non-Public ☐ P/Known *or* ☐ MISC

ADDRESS: _____

PHONE C / H / W: _____

☐ Driver's License ☐ Passport ☐ Other ID # ___ AGENCY ___ ISSUED ___ EXPIRES ___

SIGNATURE ☐ (after oath / affirmation) ❷

COMMISSION #:

Entry 11

SERVICE	DATE ___ - ___ -20___ TIME ___ : ___ am / pm ADDRESS ☐ Office NOTES
	TYPE ☐ Stop MILES ___ ☐ Adv. Travel ☐ Rush ☐ Copy ☐ Other TOTAL FEES
	$ ___ $ ___ $ ___ $ ___ $ ___
	☐ Acknowledgment ☐ Jurat ☐ Signature Witnessing ☐ Copy Certification ☐ Oath/Affirmation ☐ Notary ☐ Protest ☐ Other
DOCUMENT	DOC TYPE ☐ Deed G/QC/W ☐ DOT/Mortgage ☐ Trust Rev/Irrev/Cert ☐ Will ☐ POAF G/L D/S ☐ POAH/AHCD ☐ Affidavit ☐ Oath of Office ☐ Other
	DOC DATE J F M A M J / J A S O N D , DOC TITLE or TYPE # OF PAGES ___ ☐ Inspect/Copy Request Entry X-Ref #
SIGNER	☐ **SATISFACTORY EVIDENCE** ☐ Driver's License / Passport / Other ID *or* ☐ Credible Witness(es) *OR* ☐ Personal Knowledge
	SIGNER's NAME ☐ For ☐ Non-Public ☐ Driver's License ☐ Passport ☐ Other ID ISSUED ___ EXPIRES ___ SIGNATURE ☐ (oath/affirmation, if any) ☐ (by Mark)
	PHONE C / H / W ___ / ___ ADDRESS # ___ AGENCY ___
CW #1	#1 WITNESS's NAME ☐ P/Known ☐ Non-Public ☐ Driver's License ☐ Passport ☐ Other ID ISSUED ___ EXPIRES ___ SIGNATURE ☐ (after oath / affirmation) ❶
	PHONE C / H / W ___ / ___ *or* ☐ MISC ADDRESS # ___ AGENCY ___
CW #2	#2 WITNESS's NAME ☐ P/Known ☐ Non-Public ☐ Driver's License ☐ Passport ☐ Other ID ISSUED ___ EXPIRES ___ SIGNATURE ☐ (after oath / affirmation) ❷
	PHONE C / H / W ___ / ___ *or* ☐ MISC ADDRESS # ___ AGENCY ___

Fingerprint R T I M R P L

Entry 12

SERVICE	DATE ___ - ___ -20___ TIME ___ : ___ am / pm ADDRESS ☐ Office NOTES
	TYPE ☐ Stop MILES ___ ☐ Adv. Travel ☐ Rush ☐ Copy ☐ Other TOTAL FEES
	$ ___ $ ___ $ ___ $ ___ $ ___
	☐ Acknowledgment ☐ Jurat ☐ Signature Witnessing ☐ Copy Certification ☐ Oath/Affirmation ☐ Notary ☐ Protest ☐ Other
DOCUMENT	DOC TYPE ☐ Deed G/QC/W ☐ DOT/Mortgage ☐ Trust Rev/Irrev/Cert ☐ Will ☐ POAF G/L D/S ☐ POAH/AHCD ☐ Affidavit ☐ Oath of Office ☐ Other
	DOC DATE J F M A M J / J A S O N D , DOC TITLE or TYPE # OF PAGES ___ ☐ Inspect/Copy Request Entry X-Ref #
SIGNER	☐ **SATISFACTORY EVIDENCE** ☐ Driver's License / Passport / Other ID *or* ☐ Credible Witness(es) *OR* ☐ Personal Knowledge
	SIGNER's NAME ☐ For ☐ Non-Public ☐ Driver's License ☐ Passport ☐ Other ID ISSUED ___ EXPIRES ___ SIGNATURE ☐ (oath/affirmation, if any) ☐ (by Mark)
	PHONE C / H / W ___ / ___ ADDRESS # ___ AGENCY ___
CW #1	#1 WITNESS's NAME ☐ P/Known ☐ Non-Public ☐ Driver's License ☐ Passport ☐ Other ID ISSUED ___ EXPIRES ___ SIGNATURE ☐ (after oath / affirmation) ❶
	PHONE C / H / W ___ / ___ *or* ☐ MISC ADDRESS # ___ AGENCY ___
CW #2	#2 WITNESS's NAME ☐ P/Known ☐ Non-Public ☐ Driver's License ☐ Passport ☐ Other ID ISSUED ___ EXPIRES ___ SIGNATURE ☐ (after oath / affirmation) ❷
	PHONE C / H / W ___ / ___ *or* ☐ MISC ADDRESS # ___ AGENCY ___

Fingerprint R T I M R P L

COMMISSION #:

NOTARY NAME (printed): _____

Entry 13

13	Fingerprint

DATE ___ - ___ -20___   TIME ___ : ___ am/pm   ☐ Office   NOTES

☐ Stop ☐ MILES ☐ Notary ☐ Adv. Travel ☐ Rush ☐ Copy ☐ Other TOTAL FEES
$___ $___ $___ $___ $___ $___ $___

R
T
I
M
R
P
L

SERVICE — TYPE ☐ Acknowledgment ☐ Jurat ☐ Signature Witnessing ☐ Copy Certification ☐ Oath/Affirmation ☐ Oath of Office ☐ Protest ☐ Other

DOCUMENT — DOC TYPE ☐ Deed G/QC/W ☐ DOT/Mortgage ☐ Trust Rev/Irrev/Cert ☐ Will ☐ POAF G/L D/S ☐ POAH/AHCD ☐ Affidavit ☐ Other

DOC DATE J F M A M J / J A S O N D , ___   DOC TITLE or TYPE ___   # OF PAGES ___   ☐ Inspect/Copy Request   Entry X-Ref #

SIGNER — ☐ SATISFACTORY EVIDENCE ☐ Driver's License / Passport / Other ID   or   ☐ Credible Witness(es)   OR   ☐ Personal Knowledge

SIGNER's NAME ___   ☐ For ☐ Non-Public   ☐ Driver's License ☐ Passport ☐ Other ID ISSUED ___ EXPIRES ___   SIGNATURE ☐ (oath/affirmation, if any) ☐ (by Mark)
ADDRESS ___
PHONE C / H / W ___   or ☐ MISC   # ___ AGENCY ___

CW #1 — #1 WITNESS's NAME ___   ☐ P/Known ☐ Non-Public   ☐ Driver's License ☐ Passport ☐ Other ID ISSUED ___ EXPIRES ___   SIGNATURE ☐ (after oath / affirmation) ❶
ADDRESS ___
PHONE C / H / W ___   or ☐ MISC   # ___ AGENCY ___

CW #2 — #2 WITNESS's NAME ___   ☐ P/Known ☐ Non-Public   ☐ Driver's License ☐ Passport ☐ Other ID ISSUED ___ EXPIRES ___   SIGNATURE ☐ (after oath / affirmation) ❷
ADDRESS ___
PHONE C / H / W ___   or ☐ MISC   # ___ AGENCY ___

Entry 14

14	Fingerprint

DATE ___ - ___ -20___   TIME ___ : ___ am/pm   ☐ Office   NOTES

☐ Stop ☐ MILES ☐ Notary ☐ Adv. Travel ☐ Rush ☐ Copy ☐ Other TOTAL FEES
$___ $___ $___ $___ $___ $___ $___

R
T
I
M
R
P
L

SERVICE — TYPE ☐ Acknowledgment ☐ Jurat ☐ Signature Witnessing ☐ Copy Certification ☐ Oath/Affirmation ☐ Oath of Office ☐ Protest ☐ Other

DOCUMENT — DOC TYPE ☐ Deed G/QC/W ☐ DOT/Mortgage ☐ Trust Rev/Irrev/Cert ☐ Will ☐ POAF G/L D/S ☐ POAH/AHCD ☐ Affidavit ☐ Other

DOC DATE J F M A M J / J A S O N D , ___   DOC TITLE or TYPE ___   # OF PAGES ___   ☐ Inspect/Copy Request   Entry X-Ref #

SIGNER — ☐ SATISFACTORY EVIDENCE ☐ Driver's License / Passport / Other ID   or   ☐ Credible Witness(es)   OR   ☐ Personal Knowledge

SIGNER's NAME ___   ☐ For ☐ Non-Public   ☐ Driver's License ☐ Passport ☐ Other ID ISSUED ___ EXPIRES ___   SIGNATURE ☐ (oath/affirmation, if any) ☐ (by Mark)
ADDRESS ___
PHONE C / H / W ___   or ☐ MISC   # ___ AGENCY ___

CW #1 — #1 WITNESS's NAME ___   ☐ P/Known ☐ Non-Public   ☐ Driver's License ☐ Passport ☐ Other ID ISSUED ___ EXPIRES ___   SIGNATURE ☐ (after oath / affirmation) ❶
ADDRESS ___
PHONE C / H / W ___   or ☐ MISC   # ___ AGENCY ___

CW #2 — #2 WITNESS's NAME ___   ☐ P/Known ☐ Non-Public   ☐ Driver's License ☐ Passport ☐ Other ID ISSUED ___ EXPIRES ___   SIGNATURE ☐ (after oath / affirmation) ❷
ADDRESS ___
PHONE C / H / W ___   or ☐ MISC   # ___ AGENCY ___

NOTARY NAME (printed): _____   COMMISSION #: _____

Entry 15

SERVICE								TOTAL FEES
□ Office	□ Stop	MILES	□ Notary	□ Adv. Travel	□ Rush	□ Copy	□ Other	$

DATE ____ - ____ -20____   TIME ____ : ____ am pm   ADDRESS _____   NOTES _____

Fingerprint
R — T — I — M — R — P — L

SERVICE TYPE: □ Acknowledgment □ Jurat □ Signature Witnessing □ Copy Certification □ Oath/Affirmation □ Oath of Office □ Protest □ Other

DOCUMENT
DOC TYPE: □ Deed G/QC/W □ DOT/Mortgage □ Trust Rev/Irrev/Cert □ Will □ POAF G/L D/S □ POAH/AHCD □ Affidavit □ Other
DOC DATE J F M A M J J A S O N D , ____   DOC TITLE or TYPE ____
OF PAGES ____   □ Inspect/Copy Request   Entry X-Ref # ____

SIGNER
□ SATISFACTORY EVIDENCE   □ Personal Knowledge   OR   □ Driver's License / Passport / Other ID   or   □ Credible Witness(es)
SIGNER's NAME ____   □ For □ Non-Public   ADDRESS ____   □ Driver's License □ Passport □ Other ID   ISSUED ____   SIGNATURE ____ □ (oath/affirmation, if any) □ (by Mark)
PHONE C / H / W ____ / ____   or □ MISC ____   # ____ AGENCY ____   EXPIRES ____

CW #1
#1 WITNESS's NAME ____   □ P/Known   ADDRESS ____   □ Driver's License □ Passport □ Other ID   ISSUED ____   SIGNATURE ____ □ (after oath / affirmation) ❶
PHONE C / H / W ____ / ____   or □ MISC ____   # ____ AGENCY ____   EXPIRES ____

CW #2
#2 WITNESS's NAME ____   □ P/Known   ADDRESS ____   □ Driver's License □ Passport □ Other ID   ISSUED ____   SIGNATURE ____ □ (after oath / affirmation) ❷
PHONE C / H / W ____ / ____   or □ MISC ____   # ____ AGENCY ____   EXPIRES ____

Entry 16

SERVICE								TOTAL FEES
□ Office	□ Stop	MILES	□ Notary	□ Adv. Travel	□ Rush	□ Copy	□ Other	$

DATE ____ - ____ -20____   TIME ____ : ____ am pm   ADDRESS _____   NOTES _____

Fingerprint
R — T — I — M — R — P — L

SERVICE TYPE: □ Acknowledgment □ Jurat □ Signature Witnessing □ Copy Certification □ Oath/Affirmation □ Oath of Office □ Protest □ Other

DOCUMENT
DOC TYPE: □ Deed G/QC/W □ DOT/Mortgage □ Trust Rev/Irrev/Cert □ Will □ POAF G/L D/S □ POAH/AHCD □ Affidavit □ Other
DOC DATE J F M A M J J A S O N D , ____   DOC TITLE or TYPE ____
OF PAGES ____   □ Inspect/Copy Request   Entry X-Ref # ____

SIGNER
□ SATISFACTORY EVIDENCE   □ Personal Knowledge   OR   □ Driver's License / Passport / Other ID   or   □ Credible Witness(es)
SIGNER's NAME ____   □ For □ Non-Public   ADDRESS ____   □ Driver's License □ Passport □ Other ID   ISSUED ____   SIGNATURE ____ □ (oath/affirmation, if any) □ (by Mark)
PHONE C / H / W ____ / ____   or □ MISC ____   # ____ AGENCY ____   EXPIRES ____

CW #1
#1 WITNESS's NAME ____   □ P/Known   ADDRESS ____   □ Driver's License □ Passport □ Other ID   ISSUED ____   SIGNATURE ____ □ (after oath / affirmation) ❶
PHONE C / H / W ____ / ____   or □ MISC ____   # ____ AGENCY ____   EXPIRES ____

CW #2
#2 WITNESS's NAME ____   □ P/Known   ADDRESS ____   □ Driver's License □ Passport □ Other ID   ISSUED ____   SIGNATURE ____ □ (after oath / affirmation) ❷
PHONE C / H / W ____ / ____   or □ MISC ____   # ____ AGENCY ____   EXPIRES ____

NOTARY NAME (printed): _____ COMMISSION #: _____

Entry 17

SERVICE

DATE: ___ - ___ -20___ TIME: ___ : ___ ☐ am ☐ pm ADDRESS _____ ☐ Office NOTES _____

☐ Stop ┊ MILES ┊ ☐ Notary ☐ Adv. Travel ☐ Rush ☐ Copy ☐ Other TOTAL FEES

$ ____ $ ____ $ ____ $ ____ $ ____ $ ____

Fingerprint

R
T
I
M
R
P
L

DOCUMENT

TYPE: ☐ Acknowledgment ☐ Jurat ☐ Signature Witnessing ☐ Copy Certification ☐ Oath/Affirmation ☐ Oath of Office ☐ Protest ☐ Other

DOC TYPE: ☐ Deed G/QC/W ☐ DOT/Mortgage ☐ Trust Rev/Irrev/Cert ☐ Will ☐ POAF G/L D/S ☐ POAH/AHCD ☐ Affidavit ☐ Other

DOC DATE: J F M A M J J A S O N D , _____ # OF PAGES ____ ☐ Inspect/Copy Request Entry X-Ref # ____

DOC TITLE or TYPE _____

SIGNER

☐ SATISFACTORY EVIDENCE ☐ Driver's License / Passport / Other ID **or** ☐ Credible Witness(es) **OR** ☐ Personal Knowledge

☐ For ☐ Non-Public ☐ Driver's License ☐ Passport ☐ Other ID ISSUED ____ SIGNATURE ☐ (oath/affirmation, if any) ☐ (by Mark)

SIGNER's NAME _____ ADDRESS _____

PHONE C / H / W ____ / ____ **or** ☐ MISC # ____ AGENCY ____ EXPIRES ____

⬆

CW #1

☐ P/Known ☐ Non-Public ☐ Driver's License ☐ Passport ☐ Other ID ISSUED ____ SIGNATURE ☐ (after oath / affirmation)

#1 WITNESS's NAME _____ ADDRESS _____

PHONE C / H / W ____ / ____ **or** ☐ MISC # ____ AGENCY ____ EXPIRES ____

❶

CW #2

☐ P/Known ☐ Non-Public ☐ Driver's License ☐ Passport ☐ Other ID ISSUED ____ SIGNATURE ☐ (after oath / affirmation)

#2 WITNESS's NAME _____ ADDRESS _____

PHONE C / H / W ____ / ____ **or** ☐ MISC # ____ AGENCY ____ EXPIRES ____

❷

Entry 18

SERVICE

DATE: ___ - ___ -20___ TIME: ___ : ___ ☐ am ☐ pm ADDRESS _____ ☐ Office NOTES _____

☐ Stop ┊ MILES ┊ ☐ Notary ☐ Adv. Travel ☐ Rush ☐ Copy ☐ Other TOTAL FEES

$ ____ $ ____ $ ____ $ ____ $ ____ $ ____

Fingerprint

R
T
I
M
R
P
L

DOCUMENT

TYPE: ☐ Acknowledgment ☐ Jurat ☐ Signature Witnessing ☐ Copy Certification ☐ Oath/Affirmation ☐ Oath of Office ☐ Protest ☐ Other

DOC TYPE: ☐ Deed G/QC/W ☐ DOT/Mortgage ☐ Trust Rev/Irrev/Cert ☐ Will ☐ POAF G/L D/S ☐ POAH/AHCD ☐ Affidavit ☐ Other

DOC DATE: J F M A M J J A S O N D , _____ # OF PAGES ____ ☐ Inspect/Copy Request Entry X-Ref # ____

DOC TITLE or TYPE _____

SIGNER

☐ SATISFACTORY EVIDENCE ☐ Driver's License / Passport / Other ID **or** ☐ Credible Witness(es) **OR** ☐ Personal Knowledge

☐ For ☐ Non-Public ☐ Driver's License ☐ Passport ☐ Other ID ISSUED ____ SIGNATURE ☐ (oath/affirmation, if any) ☐ (by Mark)

SIGNER's NAME _____ ADDRESS _____

PHONE C / H / W ____ / ____ **or** ☐ MISC # ____ AGENCY ____ EXPIRES ____

⬆

CW #1

☐ P/Known ☐ Non-Public ☐ Driver's License ☐ Passport ☐ Other ID ISSUED ____ SIGNATURE ☐ (after oath / affirmation)

#1 WITNESS's NAME _____ ADDRESS _____

PHONE C / H / W ____ / ____ **or** ☐ MISC # ____ AGENCY ____ EXPIRES ____

❶

CW #2

☐ P/Known ☐ Non-Public ☐ Driver's License ☐ Passport ☐ Other ID ISSUED ____ SIGNATURE ☐ (after oath / affirmation)

#2 WITNESS's NAME _____ ADDRESS _____

PHONE C / H / W ____ / ____ **or** ☐ MISC # ____ AGENCY ____ EXPIRES ____

❷

COMMISSION #:

NOTARY NAME (printed):

Entry 19

| SERVICE | DOCUMENT | SIGNER | CW #1 | CW #2 |

19

☐ Stop ☐ MILES ☐ Adv. Travel ☐ Rush ☐ Copy ☐ Other TOTAL FEES
☐ Office NOTES
$ $ $ $ $ $

SERVICE
DATE ___ - ___ -20   TIME ___ : ___ ☐ am ☐ pm   ADDRESS
TYPE ☐ Acknowledgment ☐ Jurat ☐ Signature Witnessing ☐ Copy Certification ☐ Oath/Affirmation ☐ Oath of Office ☐ Protest ☐ Other

DOCUMENT
DOC TYPE ☐ Deed G/QC/W ☐ DOT/Mortgage ☐ Trust Rev/Irrev/Cert ☐ Will ☐ POAF G/L D/S ☐ POAH/AHCD ☐ Affidavit ☐ Other
DOC DATE J F M A M J / J A S O N D ,   DOC TITLE or TYPE
OF PAGES ☐ Inspect/Copy Request   Entry X-Ref

SIGNER
☐ SATISFACTORY EVIDENCE ☐ Driver's License / Passport / Other ID *or* ☐ Credible Witness(es) **OR** ☐ Personal Knowledge
SIGNER's NAME
☐ For ☐ Non-Public ☐ Driver's License ☐ Passport ☐ Other ID ISSUED ___ EXPIRES ___ ADDRESS
or ☐ MISC # AGENCY
PHONE C / H / W ___ / ___
SIGNATURE ☐ (oath/affirmation, if any) ☐ (by Mark)

CW #1
#1 WITNESS's NAME
☐ P/Known ☐ Non-Public ☐ Driver's License ☐ Passport ☐ Other ID ISSUED ___ EXPIRES ___ ADDRESS
or ☐ MISC # AGENCY
PHONE C / H / W ___ / ___
SIGNATURE ☐ (after oath / affirmation) ❶

CW #2
#2 WITNESS's NAME
☐ P/Known ☐ Non-Public ☐ Driver's License ☐ Passport ☐ Other ID ISSUED ___ EXPIRES ___ ADDRESS
or ☐ MISC # AGENCY
PHONE C / H / W ___ / ___
SIGNATURE ☐ (after oath / affirmation) ❷

Fingerprint
R T I M R P L

Entry 20

20

☐ Stop ☐ MILES ☐ Adv. Travel ☐ Rush ☐ Copy ☐ Other TOTAL FEES
☐ Office NOTES
$ $ $ $ $ $

SERVICE
DATE ___ - ___ -20   TIME ___ : ___ ☐ am ☐ pm   ADDRESS
TYPE ☐ Acknowledgment ☐ Jurat ☐ Signature Witnessing ☐ Copy Certification ☐ Oath/Affirmation ☐ Oath of Office ☐ Protest ☐ Other

DOCUMENT
DOC TYPE ☐ Deed G/QC/W ☐ DOT/Mortgage ☐ Trust Rev/Irrev/Cert ☐ Will ☐ POAF G/L D/S ☐ POAH/AHCD ☐ Affidavit ☐ Other
DOC DATE J F M A M J / J A S O N D ,   DOC TITLE or TYPE
OF PAGES ☐ Inspect/Copy Request   Entry X-Ref

SIGNER
☐ SATISFACTORY EVIDENCE ☐ Driver's License / Passport / Other ID *or* ☐ Credible Witness(es) **OR** ☐ Personal Knowledge
SIGNER's NAME
☐ For ☐ Non-Public ☐ Driver's License ☐ Passport ☐ Other ID ISSUED ___ EXPIRES ___ ADDRESS
or ☐ MISC # AGENCY
PHONE C / H / W ___ / ___
SIGNATURE ☐ (oath/affirmation, if any) ☐ (by Mark)

CW #1
#1 WITNESS's NAME
☐ P/Known ☐ Non-Public ☐ Driver's License ☐ Passport ☐ Other ID ISSUED ___ EXPIRES ___ ADDRESS
or ☐ MISC # AGENCY
PHONE C / H / W ___ / ___
SIGNATURE ☐ (after oath / affirmation) ❶

CW #2
#2 WITNESS's NAME
☐ P/Known ☐ Non-Public ☐ Driver's License ☐ Passport ☐ Other ID ISSUED ___ EXPIRES ___ ADDRESS
or ☐ MISC # AGENCY
PHONE C / H / W ___ / ___
SIGNATURE ☐ (after oath / affirmation) ❷

Fingerprint
R T I M R P L

Entry 21

Fingerprint
R
T
I
M
R
P
L

☐ Office

SERVICE	☐ Stop	MILES	☐ Notary	☐ Adv. Travel	☐ Rush	☐ Copy	☐ Other	TOTAL FEES
		$	$	$	$	$	$	$

DATE: __ - __ -20 __   TIME: __ : __ am/pm   ADDRESS: _____

TYPE: ☐ Acknowledgment ☐ Jurat ☐ Signature Witnessing ☐ Copy Certification ☐ Oath/Affirmation ☐ Oath of Office ☐ Protest ☐ Other

DOCUMENT
DOC TYPE: ☐ Deed G/QC/W ☐ DOT/Mortgage ☐ Trust Rev/Irrev/Cert ☐ Will ☐ POAF G/L D/S ☐ POAH/AHCD ☐ Affidavit ☐ Other
DOC DATE __ - __ J F M A M J J A S O N D   DOC TITLE or TYPE: _____
OF PAGES ____ ☐ Inspect/Copy Request Entry X-Ref # ____

NOTES: _____

SIGNER
SATISFACTORY EVIDENCE ☐ Driver's License / Passport / Other ID *or* ☐ Credible Witness(es) **OR** ☐ Personal Knowledge
SIGNER's NAME _____ ☐ For ☐ Non-Public ADDRESS _____
☐ Driver's License ☐ Passport ☐ Other ID ISSUED ____
____ *or* ☐ MISC ____ AGENCY ____ EXPIRES ____
PHONE C / H / W ____ / ____ SIGNATURE ☐ (oath/affirmation, if any) ☐ (by Mark) ⬆

CW #1
#1 WITNESS's NAME _____ ☐ P/Known ☐ Non-Public ADDRESS _____
☐ Driver's License ☐ Passport ☐ Other ID ISSUED ____
____ *or* ☐ MISC ____ AGENCY ____ EXPIRES ____
PHONE C / H / W ____ / ____ SIGNATURE ☐ (after oath / affirmation) ❶

CW #2
#2 WITNESS's NAME _____ ☐ P/Known ☐ Non-Public ADDRESS _____
☐ Driver's License ☐ Passport ☐ Other ID ISSUED ____
____ *or* ☐ MISC ____ AGENCY ____ EXPIRES ____
PHONE C / H / W ____ / ____ SIGNATURE ☐ (after oath / affirmation) ❷

Entry 22

Fingerprint
R
T
I
M
R
P
L

☐ Office

SERVICE	☐ Stop	MILES	☐ Notary	☐ Adv. Travel	☐ Rush	☐ Copy	☐ Other	TOTAL FEES
		$	$	$	$	$	$	$

DATE: __ - __ -20 __   TIME: __ : __ am/pm   ADDRESS: _____

TYPE: ☐ Acknowledgment ☐ Jurat ☐ Signature Witnessing ☐ Copy Certification ☐ Oath/Affirmation ☐ Oath of Office ☐ Protest ☐ Other

DOCUMENT
DOC TYPE: ☐ Deed G/QC/W ☐ DOT/Mortgage ☐ Trust Rev/Irrev/Cert ☐ Will ☐ POAF G/L D/S ☐ POAH/AHCD ☐ Affidavit ☐ Other
DOC DATE __ - __ J F M A M J J A S O N D   DOC TITLE or TYPE: _____
OF PAGES ____ ☐ Inspect/Copy Request Entry X-Ref # ____

NOTES: _____

SIGNER
SATISFACTORY EVIDENCE ☐ Driver's License / Passport / Other ID *or* ☐ Credible Witness(es) **OR** ☐ Personal Knowledge
SIGNER's NAME _____ ☐ For ☐ Non-Public ADDRESS _____
☐ Driver's License ☐ Passport ☐ Other ID ISSUED ____
____ *or* ☐ MISC ____ AGENCY ____ EXPIRES ____
PHONE C / H / W ____ / ____ SIGNATURE ☐ (oath/affirmation, if any) ☐ (by Mark) ⬆

CW #1
#1 WITNESS's NAME _____ ☐ P/Known ☐ Non-Public ADDRESS _____
☐ Driver's License ☐ Passport ☐ Other ID ISSUED ____
____ *or* ☐ MISC ____ AGENCY ____ EXPIRES ____
PHONE C / H / W ____ / ____ SIGNATURE ☐ (after oath / affirmation) ❶

CW #2
#2 WITNESS's NAME _____ ☐ P/Known ☐ Non-Public ADDRESS _____
☐ Driver's License ☐ Passport ☐ Other ID ISSUED ____
____ *or* ☐ MISC ____ AGENCY ____ EXPIRES ____
PHONE C / H / W ____ / ____ SIGNATURE ☐ (after oath / affirmation) ❷

NOTARY NAME (printed): _____

Entry 23

23						

☐ Stop ☐ Adv. Travel ☐ Rush ☐ Copy ☐ Other TOTAL FEES

Fingerprint

R ____ $
T
I
M ____ $
R
P
L ____ $

MILES | Notary | ____ $

SERVICE
- DATE ____ - ____ -20____
- TIME ____ : ____ am/pm
- ☐ Office NOTES
- ADDRESS

TYPE: ☐ Acknowledgment ☐ Jurat ☐ Signature Witnessing ☐ Copy Certification ☐ Oath/Affirmation ☐ Oath of Office ☐ Protest ☐ Other

DOCUMENT
- DOC TYPE: ☐ Deed G/QC/W ☐ DOT/Mortgage ☐ Trust Rev/Irrev/Cert ☐ Will ☐ POAF G/L D/S ☐ POAH/AHCD ☐ Affidavit ☐ Other
- DOC DATE: J F M A M J J A S O N D , ____
- DOC TITLE or TYPE
- # OF PAGES ☐ Inspect/Copy Request Entry X-Ref #

SIGNER
☐ **SATISFACTORY EVIDENCE** ☐ Driver's License / Passport / Other ID *or* ☐ Personal Knowledge **OR** ☐ Credible Witness(es)
- SIGNER's NAME
- ☐ For ☐ Non-Public ADDRESS
- PHONE C / H / W ____ / ____ *or* ☐ MISC
- ☐ Driver's License ☐ Passport ☐ Other ID ISSUED ____ EXPIRES ____
- # ____ AGENCY
- SIGNATURE ☐ (oath/affirmation, if any) ☐ (by Mark)

CW #1 ❶
- #1 WITNESS's NAME
- ☐ P/Known ADDRESS
- PHONE C / H / W ____ / ____ *or* ☐ MISC
- ☐ Driver's License ☐ Passport ☐ Other ID ISSUED ____ EXPIRES ____
- # ____ AGENCY
- SIGNATURE ☐ (after oath / affirmation)

CW #2 ❷
- #2 WITNESS's NAME
- ☐ P/Known ADDRESS
- PHONE C / H / W ____ / ____ *or* ☐ MISC
- ☐ Driver's License ☐ Passport ☐ Other ID ISSUED ____ EXPIRES ____
- # ____ AGENCY
- SIGNATURE ☐ (after oath / affirmation)

Entry 24

24						

☐ Stop ☐ Adv. Travel ☐ Rush ☐ Copy ☐ Other TOTAL FEES

Fingerprint

R ____ $
T
I
M ____ $
R
P
L ____ $

MILES | Notary | ____ $

SERVICE
- DATE ____ - ____ -20____
- TIME ____ : ____ am/pm
- ☐ Office NOTES
- ADDRESS

TYPE: ☐ Acknowledgment ☐ Jurat ☐ Signature Witnessing ☐ Copy Certification ☐ Oath/Affirmation ☐ Oath of Office ☐ Protest ☐ Other

DOCUMENT
- DOC TYPE: ☐ Deed G/QC/W ☐ DOT/Mortgage ☐ Trust Rev/Irrev/Cert ☐ Will ☐ POAF G/L D/S ☐ POAH/AHCD ☐ Affidavit ☐ Other
- DOC DATE: J F M A M J J A S O N D , ____
- DOC TITLE or TYPE
- # OF PAGES ☐ Inspect/Copy Request Entry X-Ref #

SIGNER
☐ **SATISFACTORY EVIDENCE** ☐ Driver's License / Passport / Other ID *or* ☐ Personal Knowledge **OR** ☐ Credible Witness(es)
- SIGNER's NAME
- ☐ For ☐ Non-Public ADDRESS
- PHONE C / H / W ____ / ____ *or* ☐ MISC
- ☐ Driver's License ☐ Passport ☐ Other ID ISSUED ____ EXPIRES ____
- # ____ AGENCY
- SIGNATURE ☐ (oath/affirmation, if any) ☐ (by Mark)

CW #1 ❶
- #1 WITNESS's NAME
- ☐ P/Known ADDRESS
- PHONE C / H / W ____ / ____ *or* ☐ MISC
- ☐ Driver's License ☐ Passport ☐ Other ID ISSUED ____ EXPIRES ____
- # ____ AGENCY
- SIGNATURE ☐ (after oath / affirmation)

CW #2 ❷
- #2 WITNESS's NAME
- ☐ P/Known ADDRESS
- PHONE C / H / W ____ / ____ *or* ☐ MISC
- ☐ Driver's License ☐ Passport ☐ Other ID ISSUED ____ EXPIRES ____
- # ____ AGENCY
- SIGNATURE ☐ (after oath / affirmation)

NOTARY NAME (printed): _____

COMMISSION #: _____

Entry 25

SERVICE

DATE __ - __ -20 | TIME __ : __ ☐ am ☐ pm | ☐ Office NOTES | ☐ Stop MILES ☐ Notary ☐ Adv. Travel ☐ Rush ☐ Copy ☐ Other TOTAL FEES
$ __ $ __ $ __ $ __ $ __ $ __ $ __

DOCUMENT

TYPE ☐ Acknowledgment ☐ Jurat ☐ Signature Witnessing ☐ Copy Certification ☐ Oath/Affirmation ☐ Oath of Office ☐ Protest ☐ Other

DOC TYPE ☐ Deed G/QC/W ☐ DOT/Mortgage ☐ Trust Rev/Irrev/Cert ☐ Will ☐ POAF G/L D/S ☐ POAH/AHCD ☐ Affidavit ☐ Other

DOC DATE J F M A M J J A S O N D , ___ DOC TITLE or TYPE ___ # OF PAGES ☐ Inspect/Copy Request Entry X-Ref #

SIGNER

SATISFACTORY EVIDENCE ☐ Driver's License / Passport / Other ID *or* ☐ Credible Witness(es) *OR* ☐ Personal Knowledge

SIGNER's NAME ___ ☐ For ADDRESS ___ ☐ Non-Public ☐ Driver's License ☐ Passport ☐ Other ID ISSUED ___

PHONE C / H / W ___ *or* ☐ MISC # ___ AGENCY ___ EXPIRES ___

SIGNATURE ☐ (oath/affirmation, if any) ☐ (by Mark) ⬆

CW #1

#1 WITNESS's NAME ___ ☐ P/Known ADDRESS ___ ☐ Non-Public ☐ Driver's License ☐ Passport ☐ Other ID ISSUED ___

PHONE C / H / W ___ *or* ☐ MISC # ___ AGENCY ___ EXPIRES ___

SIGNATURE ☐ (after oath / affirmation) ❶

CW #2

#2 WITNESS's NAME ___ ☐ P/Known ADDRESS ___ ☐ Non-Public ☐ Driver's License ☐ Passport ☐ Other ID ISSUED ___

PHONE C / H / W ___ *or* ☐ MISC # ___ AGENCY ___ EXPIRES ___

SIGNATURE ☐ (after oath / affirmation) ❷

Fingerprint
R T I M R P L

Entry 26

SERVICE

DATE __ - __ -20 | TIME __ : __ ☐ am ☐ pm | ☐ Office NOTES | ☐ Stop MILES ☐ Notary ☐ Adv. Travel ☐ Rush ☐ Copy ☐ Other TOTAL FEES
$ __ $ __ $ __ $ __ $ __ $ __ $ __

DOCUMENT

TYPE ☐ Acknowledgment ☐ Jurat ☐ Signature Witnessing ☐ Copy Certification ☐ Oath/Affirmation ☐ Oath of Office ☐ Protest ☐ Other

DOC TYPE ☐ Deed G/QC/W ☐ DOT/Mortgage ☐ Trust Rev/Irrev/Cert ☐ Will ☐ POAF G/L D/S ☐ POAH/AHCD ☐ Affidavit ☐ Other

DOC DATE J F M A M J J A S O N D , ___ DOC TITLE or TYPE ___ # OF PAGES ☐ Inspect/Copy Request Entry X-Ref #

SIGNER

SATISFACTORY EVIDENCE ☐ Driver's License / Passport / Other ID *or* ☐ Credible Witness(es) *OR* ☐ Personal Knowledge

SIGNER's NAME ___ ☐ For ADDRESS ___ ☐ Non-Public ☐ Driver's License ☐ Passport ☐ Other ID ISSUED ___

PHONE C / H / W ___ *or* ☐ MISC # ___ AGENCY ___ EXPIRES ___

SIGNATURE ☐ (oath/affirmation, if any) ☐ (by Mark) ⬆

CW #1

#1 WITNESS's NAME ___ ☐ P/Known ADDRESS ___ ☐ Non-Public ☐ Driver's License ☐ Passport ☐ Other ID ISSUED ___

PHONE C / H / W ___ *or* ☐ MISC # ___ AGENCY ___ EXPIRES ___

SIGNATURE ☐ (after oath / affirmation) ❶

CW #2

#2 WITNESS's NAME ___ ☐ P/Known ADDRESS ___ ☐ Non-Public ☐ Driver's License ☐ Passport ☐ Other ID ISSUED ___

PHONE C / H / W ___ *or* ☐ MISC # ___ AGENCY ___ EXPIRES ___

SIGNATURE ☐ (after oath / affirmation) ❷

Fingerprint
R T I M R P L

Entry 27

27

SERVICE
- DATE __ - __ -20__
- TIME __ : __ am / pm
- □ Stop □ MILES □ Adv. Travel □ Rush □ Notary □ Copy □ Other TOTAL FEES
- $ __ $ __ $ __ $ __ $ __ $ __ $ __ $ __
- □ Office NOTES
- ADDRESS

Fingerprint
R T I M R P L

DOCUMENT
- TYPE □ Acknowledgment □ Jurat □ Signature Witnessing □ Copy Certification □ Oath/Affirmation □ Oath of Office □ Protest □ Other
- DOC TYPE □ Deed G/QC/W □ DOT/Mortgage □ Trust Rev/Irrev/Cert □ Will □ POAF G/L D/S □ POAH/AHCD □ Affidavit □ Other
- DOC DATE __ J F M A M J J A S O N D , ___
- # OF PAGES __ □ Inspect/Copy Request
- Entry X-Ref # __
- DOC TITLE or TYPE

SIGNER
- SATISFACTORY EVIDENCE □ Driver's License / Passport / Other ID *or* □ Personal Knowledge □ Credible Witness(es)
- SIGNER's NAME
- PHONE C / H / W __ / __
- □ For □ Non-Public *or* □ MISC ADDRESS
- □ Driver's License □ Passport □ Other ID ISSUED __ # __ AGENCY __ EXPIRES __
- SIGNATURE □ *(oath/affirmation, if any)* □ *(by Mark)*

CW #1
- #1 WITNESS's NAME
- PHONE C / H / W __ / __
- □ P/Known *or* □ MISC ADDRESS
- □ Driver's License □ Passport □ Other ID ISSUED __ # __ AGENCY __ EXPIRES __
- SIGNATURE □ *(after oath / affirmation)* ❶

CW #2
- #2 WITNESS's NAME
- PHONE C / H / W __ / __
- □ P/Known *or* □ MISC ADDRESS
- □ Driver's License □ Passport □ Other ID ISSUED __ # __ AGENCY __ EXPIRES __
- SIGNATURE □ *(after oath / affirmation)* ❷

Entry 28

28

SERVICE
- DATE __ - __ -20__
- TIME __ : __ am / pm
- □ Stop □ MILES □ Adv. Travel □ Rush □ Notary □ Copy □ Other TOTAL FEES
- $ __ $ __ $ __ $ __ $ __ $ __ $ __ $ __
- □ Office NOTES
- ADDRESS

Fingerprint
R T I M R P L

DOCUMENT
- TYPE □ Acknowledgment □ Jurat □ Signature Witnessing □ Copy Certification □ Oath/Affirmation □ Oath of Office □ Protest □ Other
- DOC TYPE □ Deed G/QC/W □ DOT/Mortgage □ Trust Rev/Irrev/Cert □ Will □ POAF G/L D/S □ POAH/AHCD □ Affidavit □ Other
- DOC DATE __ J F M A M J J A S O N D , ___
- # OF PAGES __ □ Inspect/Copy Request
- Entry X-Ref # __
- DOC TITLE or TYPE

SIGNER
- SATISFACTORY EVIDENCE □ Driver's License / Passport / Other ID *or* □ Personal Knowledge □ Credible Witness(es)
- SIGNER's NAME
- PHONE C / H / W __ / __
- □ For □ Non-Public *or* □ MISC ADDRESS
- □ Driver's License □ Passport □ Other ID ISSUED __ # __ AGENCY __ EXPIRES __
- SIGNATURE □ *(oath/affirmation, if any)* □ *(by Mark)*

CW #1
- #1 WITNESS's NAME
- PHONE C / H / W __ / __
- □ P/Known *or* □ MISC ADDRESS
- □ Driver's License □ Passport □ Other ID ISSUED __ # __ AGENCY __ EXPIRES __
- SIGNATURE □ *(after oath / affirmation)* ❶

CW #2
- #2 WITNESS's NAME
- PHONE C / H / W __ / __
- □ P/Known *or* □ MISC ADDRESS
- □ Driver's License □ Passport □ Other ID ISSUED __ # __ AGENCY __ EXPIRES __
- SIGNATURE □ *(after oath / affirmation)* ❷

Entry 29

SERVICE

DATE ___ - ___ -20___ TIME ___:___ ☐ am ☐ pm ADDRESS _____ ☐ Office NOTES _____

☐ Stop ☐ MILES ☐ Notary ☐ Adv. Travel ☐ Rush ☐ Copy ☐ Other TOTAL FEES
$___ $___ $___ $___ $___ $___

TYPE: ☐ Acknowledgment ☐ Jurat ☐ Signature Witnessing ☐ Copy Certification ☐ Oath/Affirmation ☐ Oath of Office ☐ Protest ☐ Other

DOCUMENT

DOC TYPE: ☐ Deed G/QC/W ☐ DOT/Mortgage ☐ Trust Rev/Irrev/Cert ☐ Will ☐ POAF G/L D/S ☐ POAH/AHCD ☐ Affidavit ☐ Other

DOC DATE ___ J F M A M J J A S O N D , ___ DOC TITLE or TYPE _____ # OF PAGES ___ ☐ Inspect/Copy Request Entry X-Ref # ___

SIGNER

☐ **SATISFACTORY EVIDENCE** ☐ Driver's License / Passport / Other ID *or* ☐ Credible Witness(es) **OR** ☐ Personal Knowledge

SIGNER's NAME _____ ☐ For ☐ Non-Public ADDRESS _____ ☐ Driver's License ☐ Passport ☐ Other ID ISSUED ___ SIGNATURE _____ *(oath/affirmation, if any)*

PHONE C / H / W ___/___ *or* ☐ MISC ___ # ___ AGENCY ___ EXPIRES ___ ⬆

CW #1

#1 WITNESS's NAME _____ ☐ P/Known ADDRESS _____ ☐ Driver's License ☐ Passport ☐ Other ID ISSUED ___ SIGNATURE _____ *(after oath / affirmation)* ❶

PHONE C / H / W ___/___ *or* ☐ MISC ___ # ___ AGENCY ___ EXPIRES ___

CW #2

#2 WITNESS's NAME _____ ☐ P/Known ADDRESS _____ ☐ Driver's License ☐ Passport ☐ Other ID ISSUED ___ SIGNATURE _____ *(after oath / affirmation)* ❷

PHONE C / H / W ___/___ *or* ☐ MISC ___ # ___ AGENCY ___ EXPIRES ___

29

Fingerprint R T I M R P L ☐ (by Mark)

Entry 30

SERVICE

DATE ___ - ___ -20___ TIME ___:___ ☐ am ☐ pm ADDRESS _____ ☐ Office NOTES _____

☐ Stop ☐ MILES ☐ Notary ☐ Adv. Travel ☐ Rush ☐ Copy ☐ Other TOTAL FEES
$___ $___ $___ $___ $___ $___

TYPE: ☐ Acknowledgment ☐ Jurat ☐ Signature Witnessing ☐ Copy Certification ☐ Oath/Affirmation ☐ Oath of Office ☐ Protest ☐ Other

DOCUMENT

DOC TYPE: ☐ Deed G/QC/W ☐ DOT/Mortgage ☐ Trust Rev/Irrev/Cert ☐ Will ☐ POAF G/L D/S ☐ POAH/AHCD ☐ Affidavit ☐ Other

DOC DATE ___ J F M A M J J A S O N D , ___ DOC TITLE or TYPE _____ # OF PAGES ___ ☐ Inspect/Copy Request Entry X-Ref # ___

SIGNER

☐ **SATISFACTORY EVIDENCE** ☐ Driver's License / Passport / Other ID *or* ☐ Credible Witness(es) **OR** ☐ Personal Knowledge

SIGNER's NAME _____ ☐ For ☐ Non-Public ADDRESS _____ ☐ Driver's License ☐ Passport ☐ Other ID ISSUED ___ SIGNATURE _____ *(oath/affirmation, if any)*

PHONE C / H / W ___/___ *or* ☐ MISC ___ # ___ AGENCY ___ EXPIRES ___ ⬆

CW #1

#1 WITNESS's NAME _____ ☐ P/Known ADDRESS _____ ☐ Driver's License ☐ Passport ☐ Other ID ISSUED ___ SIGNATURE _____ *(after oath / affirmation)* ❶

PHONE C / H / W ___/___ *or* ☐ MISC ___ # ___ AGENCY ___ EXPIRES ___

CW #2

#2 WITNESS's NAME _____ ☐ P/Known ADDRESS _____ ☐ Driver's License ☐ Passport ☐ Other ID ISSUED ___ SIGNATURE _____ *(after oath / affirmation)* ❷

PHONE C / H / W ___/___ *or* ☐ MISC ___ # ___ AGENCY ___ EXPIRES ___

30

Fingerprint R T I M R P L ☐ (by Mark)

NOTARY NAME (printed):

COMMISSION #:

Entry 31

31

SERVICE	
DATE ___ - ___ -20___	TIME ___ : ___ am / pm
ADDRESS	

☐ Stop ☐ MILES ☐ Notary ☐ Adv. Travel ☐ Rush ☐ Copy ☐ Other TOTAL FEES
$ ___ $ ___ $ ___ $ ___ $ ___

☐ Office NOTES

Fingerprint
R
T
I
M
R
P
L

DOCUMENT
TYPE: ☐ Acknowledgment ☐ Jurat ☐ Signature Witnessing ☐ Copy Certification ☐ Oath/Affirmation ☐ Oath of Office ☐ Protest ☐ Other

DOC TYPE: ☐ Deed G/QC/W ☐ DOT/Mortgage ☐ Trust Rev/Irrev/Cert ☐ Will ☐ POAF G/L D/S ☐ POAH/AHCD ☐ Affidavit ☐ Other

DOC DATE J F M A M J J A S O N D ___ , ___
DOC TITLE or TYPE

OF PAGES ___ ☐ Inspect/Copy Request
Entry X-Ref # ___

SIGNER
☐ SATISFACTORY EVIDENCE ☐ Driver's License / Passport / Other ID *or* ☐ Credible Witness(es) **OR** ☐ Personal Knowledge

SIGNER's NAME ___ ☐ For ___ ☐ Non-Public ☐ Driver's License ☐ Passport ☐ Other ID ISSUED ___ EXPIRES ___
ADDRESS ___
PHONE C / H / W ___ / ___ *or* ☐ MISC ___ # ___ AGENCY ___
SIGNATURE ___ ☐ (oath/affirmation, if any) ☐ (by Mark)

CW #1
#1 WITNESS's NAME ___ ☐ P/Known ☐ Non-Public ☐ Driver's License ☐ Passport ☐ Other ID ISSUED ___ EXPIRES ___
ADDRESS ___
PHONE C / H / W ___ / ___ *or* ☐ MISC ___ # ___ AGENCY ___
SIGNATURE ___ ☐ (after oath / affirmation) ❶

CW #2
#2 WITNESS's NAME ___ ☐ P/Known ☐ Non-Public ☐ Driver's License ☐ Passport ☐ Other ID ISSUED ___ EXPIRES ___
ADDRESS ___
PHONE C / H / W ___ / ___ *or* ☐ MISC ___ # ___ AGENCY ___
SIGNATURE ___ ☐ (after oath / affirmation) ❷

Entry 32

32

SERVICE	
DATE ___ - ___ -20___	TIME ___ : ___ am / pm
ADDRESS	

☐ Stop ☐ MILES ☐ Notary ☐ Adv. Travel ☐ Rush ☐ Copy ☐ Other TOTAL FEES
$ ___ $ ___ $ ___ $ ___ $ ___

☐ Office NOTES

Fingerprint
R
T
I
M
R
P
L

DOCUMENT
TYPE: ☐ Acknowledgment ☐ Jurat ☐ Signature Witnessing ☐ Copy Certification ☐ Oath/Affirmation ☐ Oath of Office ☐ Protest ☐ Other

DOC TYPE: ☐ Deed G/QC/W ☐ DOT/Mortgage ☐ Trust Rev/Irrev/Cert ☐ Will ☐ POAF G/L D/S ☐ POAH/AHCD ☐ Affidavit ☐ Other

DOC DATE J F M A M J J A S O N D ___ , ___
DOC TITLE or TYPE

OF PAGES ___ ☐ Inspect/Copy Request
Entry X-Ref # ___

SIGNER
☐ SATISFACTORY EVIDENCE ☐ Driver's License / Passport / Other ID *or* ☐ Credible Witness(es) **OR** ☐ Personal Knowledge

SIGNER's NAME ___ ☐ For ___ ☐ Non-Public ☐ Driver's License ☐ Passport ☐ Other ID ISSUED ___ EXPIRES ___
ADDRESS ___
PHONE C / H / W ___ / ___ *or* ☐ MISC ___ # ___ AGENCY ___
SIGNATURE ___ ☐ (oath/affirmation, if any) ☐ (by Mark)

CW #1
#1 WITNESS's NAME ___ ☐ P/Known ☐ Non-Public ☐ Driver's License ☐ Passport ☐ Other ID ISSUED ___ EXPIRES ___
ADDRESS ___
PHONE C / H / W ___ / ___ *or* ☐ MISC ___ # ___ AGENCY ___
SIGNATURE ___ ☐ (after oath / affirmation) ❶

CW #2
#2 WITNESS's NAME ___ ☐ P/Known ☐ Non-Public ☐ Driver's License ☐ Passport ☐ Other ID ISSUED ___ EXPIRES ___
ADDRESS ___
PHONE C / H / W ___ / ___ *or* ☐ MISC ___ # ___ AGENCY ___
SIGNATURE ___ ☐ (after oath / affirmation) ❷

NOTARY NAME (printed): _____

COMMISSION #: _____

Entry 33

SERVICE	DATE __-__-20__ TIME __:__ am pm ADDRESS _____ Office NOTES _____
	□ Stop □ MILES $___ □ Notary $___ □ Adv. Travel $___ □ Rush $___ □ Copy $___ □ Other $___ TOTAL FEES $___
DOCUMENT	TYPE □ Acknowledgment □ Jurat □ Signature Witnessing □ Copy Certification □ Oath/Affirmation □ Oath of Office □ Protest □ Other
	DOC TYPE □ Deed G/QC/W □ DOT/Mortgage □ Trust Rev/Irrev/Cert □ Will □ POAF G/L D/S □ POAH/AHCD □ Affidavit □ Other
	DOC DATE J F M A M J J A S O N D , ____ DOC TITLE or TYPE _____ # OF PAGES ___ □ Inspect/Copy Request Entry X-Ref # ___

SATISFACTORY EVIDENCE □ Driver's License / Passport / Other ID *or* □ Credible Witness(es) *OR* □ Personal Knowledge

Fingerprint
R T I M R P L

SIGNER	
SIGNER's NAME _____	□ For ADDRESS _____ □ Non-Public □ Driver's License □ Passport □ Other ID SIGNATURE _____ □ (oath/affirmation, if any)
PHONE C / H / W ___ / ___	*or* □ MISC _____ # ___ AGENCY ___ ISSUED ___ EXPIRES ___

CW #1	
#1 WITNESS's NAME _____	□ P/Known ADDRESS _____ □ Non-Public □ Driver's License □ Passport □ Other ID SIGNATURE _____ □ (after oath / affirmation) ❶
PHONE C / H / W ___ / ___	*or* □ MISC _____ # ___ AGENCY ___ ISSUED ___ EXPIRES ___

CW #2	
#2 WITNESS's NAME _____	□ P/Known ADDRESS _____ □ Non-Public □ Driver's License □ Passport □ Other ID SIGNATURE _____ □ (after oath / affirmation) ❷
PHONE C / H / W ___ / ___	*or* □ MISC _____ # ___ AGENCY ___ ISSUED ___ EXPIRES ___

Entry 34

SERVICE	DATE __-__-20__ TIME __:__ am pm ADDRESS _____ Office NOTES _____
	□ Stop □ MILES $___ □ Notary $___ □ Adv. Travel $___ □ Rush $___ □ Copy $___ □ Other $___ TOTAL FEES $___
DOCUMENT	TYPE □ Acknowledgment □ Jurat □ Signature Witnessing □ Copy Certification □ Oath/Affirmation □ Oath of Office □ Protest □ Other
	DOC TYPE □ Deed G/QC/W □ DOT/Mortgage □ Trust Rev/Irrev/Cert □ Will □ POAF G/L D/S □ POAH/AHCD □ Affidavit □ Other
	DOC DATE J F M A M J J A S O N D , ____ DOC TITLE or TYPE _____ # OF PAGES ___ □ Inspect/Copy Request Entry X-Ref # ___

SATISFACTORY EVIDENCE □ Driver's License / Passport / Other ID *or* □ Credible Witness(es) *OR* □ Personal Knowledge

Fingerprint
R T I M R P L

SIGNER	
SIGNER's NAME _____	□ For ADDRESS _____ □ Non-Public □ Driver's License □ Passport □ Other ID SIGNATURE _____ □ (oath/affirmation, if any)
PHONE C / H / W ___ / ___	*or* □ MISC _____ # ___ AGENCY ___ ISSUED ___ EXPIRES ___

CW #1	
#1 WITNESS's NAME _____	□ P/Known ADDRESS _____ □ Non-Public □ Driver's License □ Passport □ Other ID SIGNATURE _____ □ (after oath / affirmation) ❶
PHONE C / H / W ___ / ___	*or* □ MISC _____ # ___ AGENCY ___ ISSUED ___ EXPIRES ___

CW #2	
#2 WITNESS's NAME _____	□ P/Known ADDRESS _____ □ Non-Public □ Driver's License □ Passport □ Other ID SIGNATURE _____ □ (after oath / affirmation) ❷
PHONE C / H / W ___ / ___	*or* □ MISC _____ # ___ AGENCY ___ ISSUED ___ EXPIRES ___

□ (by Mark)

NOTARY NAME (printed): _____ COMMISSION #: _____

Entry 35

SERVICE	DATE ___ - ___ -20___ TIME ___:___ ☐ am ☐ pm ADDRESS ___ ☐ Office NOTES ___ ☐ Stop ☐ MILES ___ ☐ Notary $___ ☐ Adv. Travel $___ ☐ Rush $___ ☐ Copy $___ ☐ Other $___ TOTAL FEES $___
DOCUMENT	TYPE ☐ Acknowledgment ☐ Jurat ☐ Signature Witnessing ☐ Copy Certification ☐ Oath/Affirmation ☐ Oath of Office ☐ Protest ☐ Other DOC TYPE ☐ Deed G/QC/W ☐ DOT/Mortgage ☐ Trust Rev/Irrev/Cert ☐ Will ☐ POAF G/L D/S ☐ POAH/AHCD ☐ Affidavit ☐ Other DOC DATE ___ - ___ J F M A M J J A S O N D , ___ DOC TITLE or TYPE ___ # OF PAGES ___ ☐ Inspect/Copy Request Entry X-Ref # ___
SIGNER	**SATISFACTORY EVIDENCE** ☐ Driver's License / Passport / Other ID *or* ☐ Credible Witness(es) **OR** ☐ Personal Knowledge SIGNER's NAME ___ ☐ For ☐ Non-Public ADDRESS ___ ☐ Driver's License ☐ Passport ☐ Other ID ISSUED ___ SIGNATURE ___ *(oath/affirmation, if any)* ☐ (by Mark) PHONE C / H / W ___ *or* ☐ MISC ___ # ___ AGENCY ___ EXPIRES ___
CW #1	#1 WITNESS's NAME ___ ☐ P/Known ☐ Non-Public ADDRESS ___ ☐ Driver's License ☐ Passport ☐ Other ID ISSUED ___ SIGNATURE ___ *(after oath / affirmation)* PHONE C / H / W ___ *or* ☐ MISC ___ # ___ AGENCY ___ EXPIRES ___
CW #2	#2 WITNESS's NAME ___ ☐ P/Known ☐ Non-Public ADDRESS ___ ☐ Driver's License ☐ Passport ☐ Other ID ISSUED ___ SIGNATURE ___ *(after oath / affirmation)* PHONE C / H / W ___ *or* ☐ MISC ___ # ___ AGENCY ___ EXPIRES ___

35 **Fingerprint**
R
T
I
M
R
P
L

Entry 36

SERVICE	DATE ___ - ___ -20___ TIME ___:___ ☐ am ☐ pm ADDRESS ___ ☐ Office NOTES ___ ☐ Stop ☐ MILES ___ ☐ Notary $___ ☐ Adv. Travel $___ ☐ Rush $___ ☐ Copy $___ ☐ Other $___ TOTAL FEES $___
DOCUMENT	TYPE ☐ Acknowledgment ☐ Jurat ☐ Signature Witnessing ☐ Copy Certification ☐ Oath/Affirmation ☐ Oath of Office ☐ Protest ☐ Other DOC TYPE ☐ Deed G/QC/W ☐ DOT/Mortgage ☐ Trust Rev/Irrev/Cert ☐ Will ☐ POAF G/L D/S ☐ POAH/AHCD ☐ Affidavit ☐ Other DOC DATE ___ - ___ J F M A M J J A S O N D , ___ DOC TITLE or TYPE ___ # OF PAGES ___ ☐ Inspect/Copy Request Entry X-Ref # ___
SIGNER	**SATISFACTORY EVIDENCE** ☐ Driver's License / Passport / Other ID *or* ☐ Credible Witness(es) **OR** ☐ Personal Knowledge SIGNER's NAME ___ ☐ For ☐ Non-Public ADDRESS ___ ☐ Driver's License ☐ Passport ☐ Other ID ISSUED ___ SIGNATURE ___ *(oath/affirmation, if any)* ☐ (by Mark) PHONE C / H / W ___ *or* ☐ MISC ___ # ___ AGENCY ___ EXPIRES ___
CW #1	#1 WITNESS's NAME ___ ☐ P/Known ☐ Non-Public ADDRESS ___ ☐ Driver's License ☐ Passport ☐ Other ID ISSUED ___ SIGNATURE ___ *(after oath / affirmation)* PHONE C / H / W ___ *or* ☐ MISC ___ # ___ AGENCY ___ EXPIRES ___
CW #2	#2 WITNESS's NAME ___ ☐ P/Known ☐ Non-Public ADDRESS ___ ☐ Driver's License ☐ Passport ☐ Other ID ISSUED ___ SIGNATURE ___ *(after oath / affirmation)* PHONE C / H / W ___ *or* ☐ MISC ___ # ___ AGENCY ___ EXPIRES ___

36 **Fingerprint**
R
T
I
M
R
P
L

NOTARY NAME (printed): _____

Entry 37

37

Fingerprint

R		
T		
I		
M		
R		
P		
L		

DATE ___ - ___ -20___ TIME ___ : ___ ☐ am ☐ pm ADDRESS _____ ☐ Stop MILES ___ ☐ Notary $___ ☐ Adv. Travel $___ ☐ Rush $___ ☐ Copy $___ ☐ Other $___ TOTAL FEES $___ ☐ Office NOTES

SERVICE
TYPE ☐ Acknowledgment ☐ Jurat ☐ Signature Witnessing ☐ Copy Certification ☐ Oath/Affirmation ☐ Oath of Office ☐ Protest ☐ Other

DOCUMENT
DOC TYPE ☐ Deed G/QC/W ☐ DOT/Mortgage ☐ Trust Rev/Irrev/Cert ☐ Will ☐ POAF G/L D/S ☐ POAH/AHCD ☐ Affidavit ☐ Other
DOC DATE J F M A M J J A S O N D , ____ DOC TITLE or TYPE _____ # OF PAGES ___ ☐ Inspect/Copy Request Entry X-Ref # ___

SIGNER
☐ SATISFACTORY EVIDENCE ☐ Driver's License / Passport / Other ID *or* ☐ Credible Witness(es) *OR* ☐ Personal Knowledge
SIGNER's NAME _____ ☐ For ☐ Non-Public ☐ Driver's License ☐ Passport ☐ Other ID ISSUED ___ EXPIRES ___
PHONE C / H / W ___ / ___ *or* ☐ MISC ADDRESS ____ # ___ AGENCY ___ SIGNATURE ____ ☐ (oath/affirmation, if any) ☐ (by Mark) ⬆

CW #1
#1 WITNESS's NAME _____ ☐ P/Known ☐ Non-Public ☐ Driver's License ☐ Passport ☐ Other ID ISSUED ___ EXPIRES ___
PHONE C / H / W ___ / ___ *or* ☐ MISC ADDRESS ____ # ___ AGENCY ___ SIGNATURE ____ ☐ (after oath / affirmation) ❶

CW #2
#2 WITNESS's NAME _____ ☐ P/Known ☐ Non-Public ☐ Driver's License ☐ Passport ☐ Other ID ISSUED ___ EXPIRES ___
PHONE C / H / W ___ / ___ *or* ☐ MISC ADDRESS ____ # ___ AGENCY ___ SIGNATURE ____ ☐ (after oath / affirmation) ❷

Entry 38

38

Fingerprint

R		
T		
I		
M		
R		
P		
L		

DATE ___ - ___ -20___ TIME ___ : ___ ☐ am ☐ pm ADDRESS _____ ☐ Stop MILES ___ ☐ Notary $___ ☐ Adv. Travel $___ ☐ Rush $___ ☐ Copy $___ ☐ Other $___ TOTAL FEES $___ ☐ Office NOTES

SERVICE
TYPE ☐ Acknowledgment ☐ Jurat ☐ Signature Witnessing ☐ Copy Certification ☐ Oath/Affirmation ☐ Oath of Office ☐ Protest ☐ Other

DOCUMENT
DOC TYPE ☐ Deed G/QC/W ☐ DOT/Mortgage ☐ Trust Rev/Irrev/Cert ☐ Will ☐ POAF G/L D/S ☐ POAH/AHCD ☐ Affidavit ☐ Other
DOC DATE J F M A M J J A S O N D , ____ DOC TITLE or TYPE _____ # OF PAGES ___ ☐ Inspect/Copy Request Entry X-Ref # ___

SIGNER
☐ SATISFACTORY EVIDENCE ☐ Driver's License / Passport / Other ID *or* ☐ Credible Witness(es) *OR* ☐ Personal Knowledge
SIGNER's NAME _____ ☐ For ☐ Non-Public ☐ Driver's License ☐ Passport ☐ Other ID ISSUED ___ EXPIRES ___
PHONE C / H / W ___ / ___ *or* ☐ MISC ADDRESS ____ # ___ AGENCY ___ SIGNATURE ____ ☐ (oath/affirmation, if any) ☐ (by Mark) ⬆

CW #1
#1 WITNESS's NAME _____ ☐ P/Known ☐ Non-Public ☐ Driver's License ☐ Passport ☐ Other ID ISSUED ___ EXPIRES ___
PHONE C / H / W ___ / ___ *or* ☐ MISC ADDRESS ____ # ___ AGENCY ___ SIGNATURE ____ ☐ (after oath / affirmation) ❶

CW #2
#2 WITNESS's NAME _____ ☐ P/Known ☐ Non-Public ☐ Driver's License ☐ Passport ☐ Other ID ISSUED ___ EXPIRES ___
PHONE C / H / W ___ / ___ *or* ☐ MISC ADDRESS ____ # ___ AGENCY ___ SIGNATURE ____ ☐ (after oath / affirmation) ❷

Entry 39

SERVICE	DATE _-_-20__ TIME _:_ ☐ am ☐ pm ADDRESS ☐ Office NOTES ☐ Stop MILES ☐ Adv. Travel $ ☐ Notary $ ☐ Rush $ ☐ Copy $ ☐ Other $ TOTAL FEES $
DOCUMENT	TYPE ☐ Acknowledgment ☐ Jurat ☐ Signature Witnessing ☐ Copy Certification ☐ Oath/Affirmation ☐ Oath of Office ☐ Protest ☐ Other DOC TYPE ☐ Deed G/QC/W ☐ DOT/Mortgage ☐ Trust Rev/Irrev/Cert ☐ Will ☐ POAF G/L D/S ☐ POAH/AHCD ☐ Affidavit ☐ Other DOC DATE J F M A M J J A S O N D , _____ DOC TITLE or TYPE ____ # OF PAGES ___ ☐ Inspect/Copy Request Entry X-Ref # ___
SIGNER	☐ SATISFACTORY EVIDENCE ☐ Driver's License / Passport / Other ID *or* ☐ Credible Witness(es) **OR** ☐ Personal Knowledge SIGNER's NAME ____ ☐ For ☐ Non-Public ADDRESS ____ ☐ Driver's License ☐ Passport ☐ Other ID ISSUED ___ SIGNATURE ☐ (oath/affirmation, if any) ☐ (by Mark) PHONE C / H / W ___ / ___ *or* ☐ MISC # ___ AGENCY ___ EXPIRES ___
CW #1	#1 WITNESS's NAME ___ ☐ P/Known ☐ Non-Public ADDRESS ___ ☐ Driver's License ☐ Passport ☐ Other ID ISSUED ___ SIGNATURE ☐ (after oath / affirmation) ❶ PHONE C / H / W ___ / ___ *or* ☐ MISC # ___ AGENCY ___ EXPIRES ___
CW #2	#2 WITNESS's NAME ___ ☐ P/Known ☐ Non-Public ADDRESS ___ ☐ Driver's License ☐ Passport ☐ Other ID ISSUED ___ SIGNATURE ☐ (after oath / affirmation) ❷ PHONE C / H / W ___ / ___ *or* ☐ MISC # ___ AGENCY ___ EXPIRES ___

39 Fingerprint R T I M R P L

Entry 40

SERVICE	DATE _-_-20__ TIME _:_ ☐ am ☐ pm ADDRESS ☐ Office NOTES ☐ Stop MILES ☐ Adv. Travel $ ☐ Notary $ ☐ Rush $ ☐ Copy $ ☐ Other $ TOTAL FEES $
DOCUMENT	TYPE ☐ Acknowledgment ☐ Jurat ☐ Signature Witnessing ☐ Copy Certification ☐ Oath/Affirmation ☐ Oath of Office ☐ Protest ☐ Other DOC TYPE ☐ Deed G/QC/W ☐ DOT/Mortgage ☐ Trust Rev/Irrev/Cert ☐ Will ☐ POAF G/L D/S ☐ POAH/AHCD ☐ Affidavit ☐ Other DOC DATE J F M A M J J A S O N D , _____ DOC TITLE or TYPE ____ # OF PAGES ___ ☐ Inspect/Copy Request Entry X-Ref # ___
SIGNER	☐ SATISFACTORY EVIDENCE ☐ Driver's License / Passport / Other ID *or* ☐ Credible Witness(es) **OR** ☐ Personal Knowledge SIGNER's NAME ____ ☐ For ☐ Non-Public ADDRESS ____ ☐ Driver's License ☐ Passport ☐ Other ID ISSUED ___ SIGNATURE ☐ (oath/affirmation, if any) ☐ (by Mark) PHONE C / H / W ___ / ___ *or* ☐ MISC # ___ AGENCY ___ EXPIRES ___
CW #1	#1 WITNESS's NAME ___ ☐ P/Known ☐ Non-Public ADDRESS ___ ☐ Driver's License ☐ Passport ☐ Other ID ISSUED ___ SIGNATURE ☐ (after oath / affirmation) ❶ PHONE C / H / W ___ / ___ *or* ☐ MISC # ___ AGENCY ___ EXPIRES ___
CW #2	#2 WITNESS's NAME ___ ☐ P/Known ☐ Non-Public ADDRESS ___ ☐ Driver's License ☐ Passport ☐ Other ID ISSUED ___ SIGNATURE ☐ (after oath / affirmation) ❷ PHONE C / H / W ___ / ___ *or* ☐ MISC # ___ AGENCY ___ EXPIRES ___

40 Fingerprint R T I M R P L

41

Fingerprint

R T I M R P L

SERVICE	□ Stop	MILES	Notary	Adv. Travel	Rush	Copy	Other	TOTAL FEES
		$	$	$	$	$	$	$

DATE ___ - ___ -20___ TIME ___ : ___ am / pm □ Office | ADDRESS | NOTES

TYPE □ Acknowledgment □ Jurat □ Signature Witnessing □ Copy Certification □ Oath/Affirmation □ Oath of Office □ Protest □ Other

DOC TYPE □ Deed G/QC/W □ DOT/Mortgage □ Trust Rev/Irrev/Cert □ Will □ POAF G/L D/S □ POAH/AHCD □ Affidavit □ Other

DOC DATE J F M A M J / J A S O N D ___ , ___   DOC TITLE or TYPE   # OF PAGES ___ □ Inspect/Copy Request   Entry X-Ref # ___

SATISFACTORY EVIDENCE □ Driver's License / Passport / Other ID *or* □ Credible Witness(es) **OR** □ Personal Knowledge

SIGNER
SIGNER's NAME
□ For □ Non-Public
□ Driver's License □ Passport □ Other ID ISSUED   EXPIRES
ADDRESS
___ AGENCY
PHONE C / H / W ___ / ___ *or* □ MISC
SIGNATURE ___ □ (oath/affirmation, if any) ↑

CW #1
#1 WITNESS's NAME
□ P/Known □ Non-Public
□ Driver's License □ Passport □ Other ID ISSUED   EXPIRES
ADDRESS
___ AGENCY
PHONE C / H / W ___ / ___ *or* □ MISC
SIGNATURE ___ □ (after oath / affirmation) ❶

CW #2
#2 WITNESS's NAME
□ P/Known □ Non-Public
□ Driver's License □ Passport □ Other ID ISSUED   EXPIRES
ADDRESS
___ AGENCY
PHONE C / H / W ___ / ___ *or* □ MISC
SIGNATURE ___ □ (after oath / affirmation) ❷

□ (by Mark)

42

Fingerprint

R T I M R P L

SERVICE	□ Stop	MILES	Notary	Adv. Travel	Rush	Copy	Other	TOTAL FEES
		$	$	$	$	$	$	$

DATE ___ - ___ -20___ TIME ___ : ___ am / pm □ Office | ADDRESS | NOTES

TYPE □ Acknowledgment □ Jurat □ Signature Witnessing □ Copy Certification □ Oath/Affirmation □ Oath of Office □ Protest □ Other

DOC TYPE □ Deed G/QC/W □ DOT/Mortgage □ Trust Rev/Irrev/Cert □ Will □ POAF G/L D/S □ POAH/AHCD □ Affidavit □ Other

DOC DATE J F M A M J / J A S O N D ___ , ___   DOC TITLE or TYPE   # OF PAGES ___ □ Inspect/Copy Request   Entry X-Ref # ___

SATISFACTORY EVIDENCE □ Driver's License / Passport / Other ID *or* □ Credible Witness(es) **OR** □ Personal Knowledge

SIGNER
SIGNER's NAME
□ For □ Non-Public
□ Driver's License □ Passport □ Other ID ISSUED   EXPIRES
ADDRESS
___ AGENCY
PHONE C / H / W ___ / ___ *or* □ MISC
SIGNATURE ___ □ (oath/affirmation, if any) ↑

CW #1
#1 WITNESS's NAME
□ P/Known □ Non-Public
□ Driver's License □ Passport □ Other ID ISSUED   EXPIRES
ADDRESS
___ AGENCY
PHONE C / H / W ___ / ___ *or* □ MISC
SIGNATURE ___ □ (after oath / affirmation) ❶

CW #2
#2 WITNESS's NAME
□ P/Known □ Non-Public
□ Driver's License □ Passport □ Other ID ISSUED   EXPIRES
ADDRESS
___ AGENCY
PHONE C / H / W ___ / ___ *or* □ MISC
SIGNATURE ___ □ (after oath / affirmation) ❷

□ (by Mark)

NOTARY NAME (printed): _____ COMMISSION #: _____

Entry 43

SERVICE
- DATE: __ - __ -20__   TIME: __ : __ ☐ am ☐ pm
- ☐ Stop ☐ MILES ☐ Adv. Travel ☐ Notary ☐ Rush ☐ Copy ☐ Other TOTAL FEES
  - $ ___ $ ___ $ ___ $ ___ $ ___ $ ___
- ☐ Office NOTES
- ADDRESS: _____

Fingerprint
R ___
T ___
I ___
M ___
R ___
P ___
L ___

DOCUMENT
- TYPE: ☐ Acknowledgment ☐ Jurat ☐ Signature Witnessing ☐ Copy Certification ☐ Oath/Affirmation ☐ Protest ☐ Other
- DOC TYPE: ☐ Deed G/QC/W ☐ DOT/Mortgage ☐ Trust Rev/Irrev/Cert ☐ Will ☐ POAF G/L D/S ☐ POAH/AHCD ☐ Affidavit ☐ Other
- DOC DATE: J F M A M J J A S O N D ___ , ___   # OF PAGES ___ ☐ Inspect/Copy Request Entry X-Ref # ___
- DOC TITLE or TYPE: _____

SIGNER
- ☐ SATISFACTORY EVIDENCE ☐ Driver's License / Passport / Other ID *or* ☐ Credible Witness(es) *OR* ☐ Personal Knowledge
- SIGNER's NAME: _____
- ☐ For ☐ Non-Public ☐ Driver's License ☐ Passport ☐ Other ID ISSUED ___ EXPIRES ___
- ADDRESS: _____
- PHONE C / H / W: ___ / ___   ☐ P/Known *or* ☐ MISC # ___ AGENCY ___
- SIGNATURE ☐ (oath/affirmation, if any) _____ ☐ (by Mark) ⬆

CW #1
- #1 WITNESS's NAME: _____
- ☐ Non-Public ☐ Driver's License ☐ Passport ☐ Other ID ISSUED ___ EXPIRES ___
- ADDRESS: _____
- PHONE C / H / W: ___ / ___   ☐ P/Known *or* ☐ MISC # ___ AGENCY ___
- SIGNATURE ☐ (after oath / affirmation) _____ ❶

CW #2
- #2 WITNESS's NAME: _____
- ☐ Non-Public ☐ Driver's License ☐ Passport ☐ Other ID ISSUED ___ EXPIRES ___
- ADDRESS: _____
- PHONE C / H / W: ___ / ___   ☐ P/Known *or* ☐ MISC # ___ AGENCY ___
- SIGNATURE ☐ (after oath / affirmation) _____ ❷

Entry 44

SERVICE
- DATE: __ - __ -20__   TIME: __ : __ ☐ am ☐ pm
- ☐ Stop ☐ MILES ☐ Adv. Travel ☐ Notary ☐ Rush ☐ Copy ☐ Other TOTAL FEES
  - $ ___ $ ___ $ ___ $ ___ $ ___ $ ___
- ☐ Office NOTES
- ADDRESS: _____

Fingerprint
R ___
T ___
I ___
M ___
R ___
P ___
L ___

DOCUMENT
- TYPE: ☐ Acknowledgment ☐ Jurat ☐ Signature Witnessing ☐ Copy Certification ☐ Oath/Affirmation ☐ Protest ☐ Other
- DOC TYPE: ☐ Deed G/QC/W ☐ DOT/Mortgage ☐ Trust Rev/Irrev/Cert ☐ Will ☐ POAF G/L D/S ☐ POAH/AHCD ☐ Affidavit ☐ Other
- DOC DATE: J F M A M J J A S O N D ___ , ___   # OF PAGES ___ ☐ Inspect/Copy Request Entry X-Ref # ___
- DOC TITLE or TYPE: _____

SIGNER
- ☐ SATISFACTORY EVIDENCE ☐ Driver's License / Passport / Other ID *or* ☐ Credible Witness(es) *OR* ☐ Personal Knowledge
- SIGNER's NAME: _____
- ☐ For ☐ Non-Public ☐ Driver's License ☐ Passport ☐ Other ID ISSUED ___ EXPIRES ___
- ADDRESS: _____
- PHONE C / H / W: ___ / ___   ☐ P/Known *or* ☐ MISC # ___ AGENCY ___
- SIGNATURE ☐ (oath/affirmation, if any) _____ ☐ (by Mark) ⬆

CW #1
- #1 WITNESS's NAME: _____
- ☐ Non-Public ☐ Driver's License ☐ Passport ☐ Other ID ISSUED ___ EXPIRES ___
- ADDRESS: _____
- PHONE C / H / W: ___ / ___   ☐ P/Known *or* ☐ MISC # ___ AGENCY ___
- SIGNATURE ☐ (after oath / affirmation) _____ ❶

CW #2
- #2 WITNESS's NAME: _____
- ☐ Non-Public ☐ Driver's License ☐ Passport ☐ Other ID ISSUED ___ EXPIRES ___
- ADDRESS: _____
- PHONE C / H / W: ___ / ___   ☐ P/Known *or* ☐ MISC # ___ AGENCY ___
- SIGNATURE ☐ (after oath / affirmation) _____ ❷

Entry 45

45   Fingerprint

SERVICE	☐ Stop	MILES	☐ Notary	☐ Adv. Travel	☐ Rush	☐ Copy	☐ Other	TOTAL FEES
DATE: ___ - ___ -20___ TIME: ___:___ ☐ am ☐ pm ☐ Office ADDRESS / NOTES	$	$	$	$	$	$	$	$

TYPE: ☐ Acknowledgment ☐ Jurat ☐ Signature Witnessing ☐ Copy Certification ☐ Oath/Affirmation ☐ Oath of Office ☐ Protest ☐ Other

DOC TYPE: ☐ Deed G/QC/W ☐ DOT/Mortgage ☐ Trust Rev/Irrev/Cert ☐ Will ☐ POAF G/L D/S ☐ POAH/AHCD ☐ Affidavit ☐ Other

DOC DATE ___ - ___ , J F M A M J J A S O N D   DOC TITLE or TYPE: ___   # OF PAGES ___   ☐ Inspect/Copy Request   Entry X-Ref # ___

SATISFACTORY EVIDENCE ☐ Driver's License / Passport / Other ID   *or*   ☐ Credible Witness(es)   *OR*   ☐ Personal Knowledge

SIGNER
SIGNER's NAME ___   ☐ For ___ *or* ☐ MISC ___   ☐ Non-Public   ☐ Driver's License ☐ Passport ☐ Other ID   ISSUED ___ EXPIRES ___   SIGNATURE ___ ☐ (oath/affirmation, if any)
PHONE C / H / W ___   # ___   AGENCY ___   R T I M R P L (Fingerprint)

CW #1
#1 WITNESS's NAME ___   ☐ P/Known *or* ☐ MISC ___   ☐ Non-Public   ☐ Driver's License ☐ Passport ☐ Other ID   ISSUED ___ EXPIRES ___   SIGNATURE ___ ❶ ☐ (after oath / affirmation)
PHONE C / H / W ___   # ___   AGENCY ___

CW #2
#2 WITNESS's NAME ___   ☐ P/Known *or* ☐ MISC ___   ☐ Non-Public   ☐ Driver's License ☐ Passport ☐ Other ID   ISSUED ___ EXPIRES ___   SIGNATURE ___ ❷ ☐ (after oath / affirmation)
PHONE C / H / W ___   # ___   AGENCY ___

☐ (by Mark)

Entry 46

46   Fingerprint

SERVICE	☐ Stop	MILES	☐ Notary	☐ Adv. Travel	☐ Rush	☐ Copy	☐ Other	TOTAL FEES
DATE: ___ - ___ -20___ TIME: ___:___ ☐ am ☐ pm ☐ Office ADDRESS / NOTES	$	$	$	$	$	$	$	$

TYPE: ☐ Acknowledgment ☐ Jurat ☐ Signature Witnessing ☐ Copy Certification ☐ Oath/Affirmation ☐ Oath of Office ☐ Protest ☐ Other

DOC TYPE: ☐ Deed G/QC/W ☐ DOT/Mortgage ☐ Trust Rev/Irrev/Cert ☐ Will ☐ POAF G/L D/S ☐ POAH/AHCD ☐ Affidavit ☐ Other

DOC DATE ___ - ___ , J F M A M J J A S O N D   DOC TITLE or TYPE: ___   # OF PAGES ___   ☐ Inspect/Copy Request   Entry X-Ref # ___

SATISFACTORY EVIDENCE ☐ Driver's License / Passport / Other ID   *or*   ☐ Credible Witness(es)   *OR*   ☐ Personal Knowledge

SIGNER
SIGNER's NAME ___   ☐ For ___ *or* ☐ MISC ___   ☐ Non-Public   ☐ Driver's License ☐ Passport ☐ Other ID   ISSUED ___ EXPIRES ___   SIGNATURE ___ ☐ (oath/affirmation, if any)
PHONE C / H / W ___   # ___   AGENCY ___   R T I M R P L (Fingerprint)

CW #1
#1 WITNESS's NAME ___   ☐ P/Known *or* ☐ MISC ___   ☐ Non-Public   ☐ Driver's License ☐ Passport ☐ Other ID   ISSUED ___ EXPIRES ___   SIGNATURE ___ ❶ ☐ (after oath / affirmation)
PHONE C / H / W ___   # ___   AGENCY ___

CW #2
#2 WITNESS's NAME ___   ☐ P/Known *or* ☐ MISC ___   ☐ Non-Public   ☐ Driver's License ☐ Passport ☐ Other ID   ISSUED ___ EXPIRES ___   SIGNATURE ___ ❷ ☐ (after oath / affirmation)
PHONE C / H / W ___   # ___   AGENCY ___

☐ (by Mark)

NOTARY NAME (printed): _____   COMMISSION #: _____

Entry 47

47 Fingerprint

	Stop	MILES	Notary	Adv. Travel	Rush	Copy	Other	TOTAL FEES
			$	$	$	$	$	$

R
T
I
M
R
P
L

SERVICE — DATE __ - __ -20__   TIME __ : __ am pm ☐ Office ADDRESS NOTES

TYPE: ☐ Acknowledgment ☐ Jurat ☐ Signature Witnessing ☐ Copy Certification ☐ Oath/Affirmation ☐ Oath of Office ☐ Protest ☐ Other

DOCUMENT
DOC TYPE: ☐ Deed G/QC/W ☐ DOT/Mortgage ☐ Trust Rev/Irrev/Cert ☐ Will ☐ POAF G/L D/S ☐ POAH/AHCD ☐ Affidavit ☐ Other
DOC DATE: J F M A M J J A S O N D , ____ DOC TITLE or TYPE
OF PAGES ____ ☐ Inspect/Copy Request Entry X-Ref

SIGNER
☐ SATISFACTORY EVIDENCE ☐ Driver's License / Passport / Other ID *or* ☐ Credible Witness(es) **OR** ☐ Personal Knowledge
SIGNER's NAME
☐ For ☐ P/Known ☐ Non-Public ☐ Driver's License ☐ Passport ☐ Other ID ISSUED ____ EXPIRES ____ SIGNATURE ☐ (oath/affirmation, if any) ☐ (by Mark)
PHONE C / H / W   /   *or* ☐ MISC # ____ AGENCY ____

CW #1
#1 WITNESS's NAME
☐ P/Known ☐ Non-Public ☐ Driver's License ☐ Passport ☐ Other ID ISSUED ____ EXPIRES ____ SIGNATURE ☐ (after oath / affirmation) ❶
PHONE C / H / W   /   *or* ☐ MISC # ____ AGENCY ____

CW #2
#2 WITNESS's NAME
☐ P/Known ☐ Non-Public ☐ Driver's License ☐ Passport ☐ Other ID ISSUED ____ EXPIRES ____ SIGNATURE ☐ (after oath / affirmation) ❷
PHONE C / H / W   /   *or* ☐ MISC # ____ AGENCY ____

Entry 48

48 Fingerprint

	Stop	MILES	Notary	Adv. Travel	Rush	Copy	Other	TOTAL FEES
			$	$	$	$	$	$

R
T
I
M
R
P
L

SERVICE — DATE __ - __ -20__   TIME __ : __ am pm ☐ Office ADDRESS NOTES

TYPE: ☐ Acknowledgment ☐ Jurat ☐ Signature Witnessing ☐ Copy Certification ☐ Oath/Affirmation ☐ Oath of Office ☐ Protest ☐ Other

DOCUMENT
DOC TYPE: ☐ Deed G/QC/W ☐ DOT/Mortgage ☐ Trust Rev/Irrev/Cert ☐ Will ☐ POAF G/L D/S ☐ POAH/AHCD ☐ Affidavit ☐ Other
DOC DATE: J F M A M J J A S O N D , ____ DOC TITLE or TYPE
OF PAGES ____ ☐ Inspect/Copy Request Entry X-Ref

SIGNER
☐ SATISFACTORY EVIDENCE ☐ Driver's License / Passport / Other ID *or* ☐ Credible Witness(es) **OR** ☐ Personal Knowledge
SIGNER's NAME
☐ For ☐ P/Known ☐ Non-Public ☐ Driver's License ☐ Passport ☐ Other ID ISSUED ____ EXPIRES ____ SIGNATURE ☐ (oath/affirmation, if any) ☐ (by Mark)
PHONE C / H / W   /   *or* ☐ MISC # ____ AGENCY ____

CW #1
#1 WITNESS's NAME
☐ P/Known ☐ Non-Public ☐ Driver's License ☐ Passport ☐ Other ID ISSUED ____ EXPIRES ____ SIGNATURE ☐ (after oath / affirmation) ❶
PHONE C / H / W   /   *or* ☐ MISC # ____ AGENCY ____

CW #2
#2 WITNESS's NAME
☐ P/Known ☐ Non-Public ☐ Driver's License ☐ Passport ☐ Other ID ISSUED ____ EXPIRES ____ SIGNATURE ☐ (after oath / affirmation) ❷
PHONE C / H / W   /   *or* ☐ MISC # ____ AGENCY ____

NOTARY NAME (printed): _____   COMMISSION #: _____

Entry 49

SERVICE	DATE __-__-20__ TIME __:__ am/pm □ Office ADDRESS NOTES	□ Stop MILES $ Notary $ □ Adv. Travel □ Rush $ □ Copy $ □ Other $ TOTAL FEES $

49

Fingerprint
R — T I M R P — L

TYPE □ Acknowledgment □ Jurat □ Signature Witnessing □ Copy Certification □ Oath/Affirmation □ Oath of Office □ Protest □ Other

DOCUMENT
DOC TYPE □ Deed G/QC/W □ DOT/Mortgage □ Trust Rev/Irrev/Cert □ Will □ POAF G/L D/S □ POAH/AHCD □ Affidavit □ Other
DOC DATE __-__-20__   J F M A M J J A S O N D
DOC TITLE or TYPE   # OF PAGES ___   □ Inspect/Copy Request   Entry X-Ref #

SATISFACTORY EVIDENCE □ Driver's License / Passport / Other ID   *or* □ Credible Witness(es)   **OR**   □ Personal Knowledge

SIGNER
SIGNER's NAME   □ For   □ Non-Public   □ Driver's License □ Passport □ Other ID   ISSUED   SIGNATURE □ (oath/affirmation, if any) □ (by Mark)
ADDRESS
PHONE C / H / W   *or* □ MISC   #   AGENCY   EXPIRES

CW #1
#1 WITNESS's NAME   □ P/Known   □ Non-Public   □ Driver's License □ Passport □ Other ID   ISSUED   SIGNATURE □ (after oath / affirmation) ❶
ADDRESS
PHONE C / H / W   *or* □ MISC   #   AGENCY   EXPIRES

CW #2
#2 WITNESS's NAME   □ P/Known   □ Non-Public   □ Driver's License □ Passport □ Other ID   ISSUED   SIGNATURE □ (after oath / affirmation) ❷
ADDRESS
PHONE C / H / W   *or* □ MISC   #   AGENCY   EXPIRES

Entry 50

SERVICE	DATE __-__-20__ TIME __:__ am/pm □ Office ADDRESS NOTES	□ Stop MILES $ Notary $ □ Adv. Travel □ Rush $ □ Copy $ □ Other $ TOTAL FEES $

50

Fingerprint
R — T I M R P — L

TYPE □ Acknowledgment □ Jurat □ Signature Witnessing □ Copy Certification □ Oath/Affirmation □ Oath of Office □ Protest □ Other

DOCUMENT
DOC TYPE □ Deed G/QC/W □ DOT/Mortgage □ Trust Rev/Irrev/Cert □ Will □ POAF G/L D/S □ POAH/AHCD □ Affidavit □ Other
DOC DATE __-__-20__   J F M A M J J A S O N D
DOC TITLE or TYPE   # OF PAGES ___   □ Inspect/Copy Request   Entry X-Ref #

SATISFACTORY EVIDENCE □ Driver's License / Passport / Other ID   *or* □ Credible Witness(es)   **OR**   □ Personal Knowledge

SIGNER
SIGNER's NAME   □ For   □ Non-Public   □ Driver's License □ Passport □ Other ID   ISSUED   SIGNATURE □ (oath/affirmation, if any) □ (by Mark)
ADDRESS
PHONE C / H / W   *or* □ MISC   #   AGENCY   EXPIRES

CW #1
#1 WITNESS's NAME   □ P/Known   □ Non-Public   □ Driver's License □ Passport □ Other ID   ISSUED   SIGNATURE □ (after oath / affirmation) ❶
ADDRESS
PHONE C / H / W   *or* □ MISC   #   AGENCY   EXPIRES

CW #2
#2 WITNESS's NAME   □ P/Known   □ Non-Public   □ Driver's License □ Passport □ Other ID   ISSUED   SIGNATURE □ (after oath / affirmation) ❷
ADDRESS
PHONE C / H / W   *or* □ MISC   #   AGENCY   EXPIRES

NOTARY NAME (printed): _____

Entry 51

COMMISSION #: _____

SERVICE	DATE ___ - ___ -20___ TIME ___ : ___ ☐ am ☐ pm ADDRESS ___ ☐ Office NOTES ___ ☐ Stop MILES ___ ☐ Notary $___ ☐ Adv. Travel $___ ☐ Rush $___ ☐ Copy $___ ☐ Other $___ TOTAL FEES $___

TYPE ☐ Acknowledgment ☐ Jurat ☐ Signature Witnessing ☐ Copy Certification ☐ Oath/Affirmation ☐ Oath of Office ☐ Protest ☐ Other

DOCUMENT
DOC TYPE ☐ Deed G/QC/W ☐ DOT/Mortgage ☐ Trust Rev/Irrev/Cert ☐ Will ☐ POAF G/L D/S ☐ POAH/AHCD ☐ Affidavit ☐ Other
DOC DATE J F M A M J J A S O N D , ___ # OF PAGES ___ ☐ Inspect/Copy Request Entry X-Ref # ___ DOC TITLE or TYPE ___

SIGNER
SATISFACTORY EVIDENCE ☐ Driver's License / Passport / Other ID *or* ☐ Credible Witness(es) **OR** ☐ Personal Knowledge
SIGNER's NAME ___ ☐ For ADDRESS ___
☐ Non-Public ☐ Driver's License ☐ Passport ☐ Other ID ISSUED ___ SIGNATURE ___ (oath/affirmation, if any) ☐ (by Mark)
PHONE C / H / W ___ / ___ *or* ☐ MISC ___ # ___ AGENCY ___ EXPIRES ___

CW #1
#1 WITNESS's NAME ___ ☐ P/Known ADDRESS ___
☐ Non-Public ☐ Driver's License ☐ Passport ☐ Other ID ISSUED ___ SIGNATURE ___ (after oath / affirmation) ❶
PHONE C / H / W ___ / ___ *or* ☐ MISC ___ # ___ AGENCY ___ EXPIRES ___

CW #2
#2 WITNESS's NAME ___ ☐ P/Known ADDRESS ___
☐ Non-Public ☐ Driver's License ☐ Passport ☐ Other ID ISSUED ___ SIGNATURE ___ (after oath / affirmation) ❷
PHONE C / H / W ___ / ___ *or* ☐ MISC ___ # ___ AGENCY ___ EXPIRES ___

Fingerprint
R T I M R P L

Entry 52

SERVICE	DATE ___ - ___ -20___ TIME ___ : ___ ☐ am ☐ pm ADDRESS ___ ☐ Office NOTES ___ ☐ Stop MILES ___ ☐ Notary $___ ☐ Adv. Travel $___ ☐ Rush $___ ☐ Copy $___ ☐ Other $___ TOTAL FEES $___

TYPE ☐ Acknowledgment ☐ Jurat ☐ Signature Witnessing ☐ Copy Certification ☐ Oath/Affirmation ☐ Oath of Office ☐ Protest ☐ Other

DOCUMENT
DOC TYPE ☐ Deed G/QC/W ☐ DOT/Mortgage ☐ Trust Rev/Irrev/Cert ☐ Will ☐ POAF G/L D/S ☐ POAH/AHCD ☐ Affidavit ☐ Other
DOC DATE J F M A M J J A S O N D , ___ # OF PAGES ___ ☐ Inspect/Copy Request Entry X-Ref # ___ DOC TITLE or TYPE ___

SIGNER
SATISFACTORY EVIDENCE ☐ Driver's License / Passport / Other ID *or* ☐ Credible Witness(es) **OR** ☐ Personal Knowledge
SIGNER's NAME ___ ☐ For ADDRESS ___
☐ Non-Public ☐ Driver's License ☐ Passport ☐ Other ID ISSUED ___ SIGNATURE ___ (oath/affirmation, if any) ☐ (by Mark)
PHONE C / H / W ___ / ___ *or* ☐ MISC ___ # ___ AGENCY ___ EXPIRES ___

CW #1
#1 WITNESS's NAME ___ ☐ P/Known ADDRESS ___
☐ Non-Public ☐ Driver's License ☐ Passport ☐ Other ID ISSUED ___ SIGNATURE ___ (after oath / affirmation) ❶
PHONE C / H / W ___ / ___ *or* ☐ MISC ___ # ___ AGENCY ___ EXPIRES ___

CW #2
#2 WITNESS's NAME ___ ☐ P/Known ADDRESS ___
☐ Non-Public ☐ Driver's License ☐ Passport ☐ Other ID ISSUED ___ SIGNATURE ___ (after oath / affirmation) ❷
PHONE C / H / W ___ / ___ *or* ☐ MISC ___ # ___ AGENCY ___ EXPIRES ___

Fingerprint
R T I M R P L

NOTARY NAME (printed): _____

COMMISSION #: _____

Entry 53

SERVICE	DATE ___ - ___ -20___ TIME ___ : ___ ☐ am ☐ pm ADDRESS ☐ Office NOTES
	☐ Stop MILES ___ Notary $___ Adv. Travel $___ Rush $___ Copy $___ Other $___ TOTAL FEES $___
DOCUMENT	TYPE ☐ Acknowledgment ☐ Jurat ☐ Signature Witnessing ☐ Copy Certification ☐ Oath/Affirmation ☐ Oath of Office ☐ Protest ☐ Other
	DOC TYPE ☐ Deed G/QC/W ☐ DOT/Mortgage ☐ Trust Rev/Irrev/Cert ☐ Will ☐ POAF G/L D/S ☐ POAH/AHCD ☐ Affidavit ☐ Other
	DOC DATE ___ J F M A M J J A S O N D , ___ DOC TITLE or TYPE # OF PAGES ___ ☐ Inspect/Copy Request Entry X-Ref # ___

Fingerprint R ☐ T I M R P L

SIGNER	☐ SATISFACTORY EVIDENCE ☐ Driver's License / Passport / Other ID *or* ☐ Credible Witness(es) *OR* ☐ Personal Knowledge
	SIGNER's NAME ___ ☐ For ADDRESS ___ ☐ Non-Public ☐ Driver's License ☐ Passport ☐ Other ID ISSUED ___ SIGNATURE ___ *(oath/affirmation, if any)* ☐ (by Mark)
	PHONE C / H / W ___ / ___ *or* ☐ MISC # ___ AGENCY ___ EXPIRES ___ SIGNATURE ___ *(after oath / affirmation)* ⬆
CW #1	#1 WITNESS's NAME ___ ☐ P/Known ADDRESS ___ ☐ Non-Public ☐ Driver's License ☐ Passport ☐ Other ID ISSUED ___ SIGNATURE ___
	PHONE C / H / W ___ / ___ *or* ☐ MISC # ___ AGENCY ___ EXPIRES ___ ❶
CW #2	#2 WITNESS's NAME ___ ☐ P/Known ADDRESS ___ ☐ Non-Public ☐ Driver's License ☐ Passport ☐ Other ID ISSUED ___ SIGNATURE ___ *(after oath / affirmation)*
	PHONE C / H / W ___ / ___ *or* ☐ MISC # ___ AGENCY ___ EXPIRES ___ ❷

Entry 54

SERVICE	DATE ___ - ___ -20___ TIME ___ : ___ ☐ am ☐ pm ADDRESS ☐ Office NOTES
	☐ Stop MILES ___ Notary $___ Adv. Travel $___ Rush $___ Copy $___ Other $___ TOTAL FEES $___
DOCUMENT	TYPE ☐ Acknowledgment ☐ Jurat ☐ Signature Witnessing ☐ Copy Certification ☐ Oath/Affirmation ☐ Oath of Office ☐ Protest ☐ Other
	DOC TYPE ☐ Deed G/QC/W ☐ DOT/Mortgage ☐ Trust Rev/Irrev/Cert ☐ Will ☐ POAF G/L D/S ☐ POAH/AHCD ☐ Affidavit ☐ Other
	DOC DATE ___ J F M A M J J A S O N D , ___ DOC TITLE or TYPE # OF PAGES ___ ☐ Inspect/Copy Request Entry X-Ref # ___

Fingerprint R ☐ T I M R P L

SIGNER	☐ SATISFACTORY EVIDENCE ☐ Driver's License / Passport / Other ID *or* ☐ Credible Witness(es) *OR* ☐ Personal Knowledge
	SIGNER's NAME ___ ☐ For ADDRESS ___ ☐ Non-Public ☐ Driver's License ☐ Passport ☐ Other ID ISSUED ___ SIGNATURE ___ *(oath/affirmation, if any)* ☐ (by Mark)
	PHONE C / H / W ___ / ___ *or* ☐ MISC # ___ AGENCY ___ EXPIRES ___ SIGNATURE ___ *(after oath / affirmation)* ⬆
CW #1	#1 WITNESS's NAME ___ ☐ P/Known ADDRESS ___ ☐ Non-Public ☐ Driver's License ☐ Passport ☐ Other ID ISSUED ___ SIGNATURE ___
	PHONE C / H / W ___ / ___ *or* ☐ MISC # ___ AGENCY ___ EXPIRES ___ ❶
CW #2	#2 WITNESS's NAME ___ ☐ P/Known ADDRESS ___ ☐ Non-Public ☐ Driver's License ☐ Passport ☐ Other ID ISSUED ___ SIGNATURE ___ *(after oath / affirmation)*
	PHONE C / H / W ___ / ___ *or* ☐ MISC # ___ AGENCY ___ EXPIRES ___ ❷

Entry 55

SERVICE

DATE ___-___-20___ TIME ___:___ ☐ am ☐ pm ADDRESS _____ ☐ Office NOTES _____

☐ Stop ☐ MILES $___ ☐ Notary $___ ☐ Adv. Travel $___ ☐ Rush $___ ☐ Copy $___ ☐ Other $___ TOTAL FEES $___

DOCUMENT

TYPE ☐ Acknowledgment ☐ Jurat ☐ Signature Witnessing ☐ Copy Certification ☐ Oath/Affirmation ☐ Oath of Office ☐ Protest ☐ Other

DOC TYPE ☐ Deed G/QC/W ☐ DOT/Mortgage ☐ Trust Rev/Irrev/Cert ☐ Will ☐ POAF G/L D/S ☐ POAH/AHCD ☐ Affidavit ☐ Other

DOC DATE ___-___-___ J F M A M J J A S O N D   DOC TITLE or TYPE _____ # OF PAGES ___ ☐ Inspect/Copy Request Entry X-Ref # ___

SIGNER

☐ SATISFACTORY EVIDENCE ☐ Driver's License / Passport / Other ID *or* ☐ Credible Witness(es) **OR** ☐ Personal Knowledge

SIGNER's NAME _____ ☐ For _____ ☐ Non-Public ☐ Driver's License ☐ Passport ☐ Other ID ISSUED ___ EXPIRES ___ SIGNATURE _____ ☐ (oath/affirmation, if any) ☐ (by Mark)

PHONE C / H / W ___ / ___ *or* ☐ MISC # ___ AGENCY ___

CW #1

#1 WITNESS's NAME _____ ☐ P/Known ADDRESS _____ ☐ Non-Public ☐ Driver's License ☐ Passport ☐ Other ID ISSUED ___ EXPIRES ___ SIGNATURE _____ ☐ (after oath / affirmation) ❶

PHONE C / H / W ___ / ___ *or* ☐ MISC # ___ AGENCY ___

CW #2

#2 WITNESS's NAME _____ ☐ P/Known ADDRESS _____ ☐ Non-Public ☐ Driver's License ☐ Passport ☐ Other ID ISSUED ___ EXPIRES ___ SIGNATURE _____ ☐ (after oath / affirmation) ❷

PHONE C / H / W ___ / ___ *or* ☐ MISC # ___ AGENCY ___

Fingerprint R L T I M R P

Entry 56

SERVICE

DATE ___-___-20___ TIME ___:___ ☐ am ☐ pm ADDRESS _____ ☐ Office NOTES _____

☐ Stop ☐ MILES $___ ☐ Notary $___ ☐ Adv. Travel $___ ☐ Rush $___ ☐ Copy $___ ☐ Other $___ TOTAL FEES $___

DOCUMENT

TYPE ☐ Acknowledgment ☐ Jurat ☐ Signature Witnessing ☐ Copy Certification ☐ Oath/Affirmation ☐ Oath of Office ☐ Protest ☐ Other

DOC TYPE ☐ Deed G/QC/W ☐ DOT/Mortgage ☐ Trust Rev/Irrev/Cert ☐ Will ☐ POAF G/L D/S ☐ POAH/AHCD ☐ Affidavit ☐ Other

DOC DATE ___-___-___ J F M A M J J A S O N D   DOC TITLE or TYPE _____ # OF PAGES ___ ☐ Inspect/Copy Request Entry X-Ref # ___

SIGNER

☐ SATISFACTORY EVIDENCE ☐ Driver's License / Passport / Other ID *or* ☐ Credible Witness(es) **OR** ☐ Personal Knowledge

SIGNER's NAME _____ ☐ For _____ ☐ Non-Public ☐ Driver's License ☐ Passport ☐ Other ID ISSUED ___ EXPIRES ___ SIGNATURE _____ ☐ (oath/affirmation, if any) ☐ (by Mark)

PHONE C / H / W ___ / ___ *or* ☐ MISC # ___ AGENCY ___

CW #1

#1 WITNESS's NAME _____ ☐ P/Known ADDRESS _____ ☐ Non-Public ☐ Driver's License ☐ Passport ☐ Other ID ISSUED ___ EXPIRES ___ SIGNATURE _____ ☐ (after oath / affirmation) ❶

PHONE C / H / W ___ / ___ *or* ☐ MISC # ___ AGENCY ___

CW #2

#2 WITNESS's NAME _____ ☐ P/Known ADDRESS _____ ☐ Non-Public ☐ Driver's License ☐ Passport ☐ Other ID ISSUED ___ EXPIRES ___ SIGNATURE _____ ☐ (after oath / affirmation) ❷

PHONE C / H / W ___ / ___ *or* ☐ MISC # ___ AGENCY ___

Fingerprint R L T I M R P

NOTARY NAME (printed): _____   COMMISSION #: _____

Entry 57

SERVICE	DATE ___-___-20___ TIME ___:___ ☐ am ☐ pm ADDRESS _____ ☐ Office NOTES _____ ☐ Stop ☐ MILES ☐ Notary ☐ Adv. Travel ☐ Rush ☐ Copy ☐ Other TOTAL FEES $___ $___ $___ $___ $___ $___ $___
DOCUMENT	TYPE ☐ Acknowledgment ☐ Jurat ☐ Signature Witnessing ☐ Copy Certification ☐ Oath/Affirmation ☐ Protest ☐ Other DOC TYPE ☐ Deed G/QC/W ☐ DOT/Mortgage ☐ Trust Rev/Irrev/Cert ☐ Will ☐ POAF G/L D/S ☐ POAH/AHCD ☐ Affidavit ☐ Other DOC DATE J F M A M J J A S O N D , ___ DOC TITLE or TYPE _____ # OF PAGES ___ ☐ Inspect/Copy Request Entry X-Ref # ___
SIGNER	☐ SATISFACTORY EVIDENCE ☐ Driver's License / Passport / Other ID **or** ☐ Credible Witness(es) **OR** ☐ Personal Knowledge SIGNER's NAME _____ ☐ For ☐ Non-Public ADDRESS _____ ☐ Driver's License ☐ Passport ☐ Other ID ISSUED ___ SIGNATURE _____ (oath/affirmation, if any) PHONE C / H / W ___ / ___ **or** ☐ MISC #___ AGENCY ___ EXPIRES ___ ↑ (by Mark)
CW #1	#1 WITNESS's NAME _____ ☐ P/Known ☐ Non-Public ADDRESS _____ ☐ Driver's License ☐ Passport ☐ Other ID ISSUED ___ SIGNATURE _____ (after oath / affirmation) PHONE C / H / W ___ / ___ **or** ☐ MISC #___ AGENCY ___ EXPIRES ___ ❶
CW #2	#2 WITNESS's NAME _____ ☐ P/Known ☐ Non-Public ADDRESS _____ ☐ Driver's License ☐ Passport ☐ Other ID ISSUED ___ SIGNATURE _____ (after oath / affirmation) PHONE C / H / W ___ / ___ **or** ☐ MISC #___ AGENCY ___ EXPIRES ___ ❷

57 Fingerprint R T I M R P L

Entry 58

SERVICE	DATE ___-___-20___ TIME ___:___ ☐ am ☐ pm ADDRESS _____ ☐ Office NOTES _____ ☐ Stop ☐ MILES ☐ Notary ☐ Adv. Travel ☐ Rush ☐ Copy ☐ Other TOTAL FEES $___ $___ $___ $___ $___ $___ $___
DOCUMENT	TYPE ☐ Acknowledgment ☐ Jurat ☐ Signature Witnessing ☐ Copy Certification ☐ Oath/Affirmation ☐ Protest ☐ Other DOC TYPE ☐ Deed G/QC/W ☐ DOT/Mortgage ☐ Trust Rev/Irrev/Cert ☐ Will ☐ POAF G/L D/S ☐ POAH/AHCD ☐ Affidavit ☐ Other DOC DATE J F M A M J J A S O N D , ___ DOC TITLE or TYPE _____ # OF PAGES ___ ☐ Inspect/Copy Request Entry X-Ref # ___
SIGNER	☐ SATISFACTORY EVIDENCE ☐ Driver's License / Passport / Other ID **or** ☐ Credible Witness(es) **OR** ☐ Personal Knowledge SIGNER's NAME _____ ☐ For ☐ Non-Public ADDRESS _____ ☐ Driver's License ☐ Passport ☐ Other ID ISSUED ___ SIGNATURE _____ (oath/affirmation, if any) PHONE C / H / W ___ / ___ **or** ☐ MISC #___ AGENCY ___ EXPIRES ___ ↑ (by Mark)
CW #1	#1 WITNESS's NAME _____ ☐ P/Known ☐ Non-Public ADDRESS _____ ☐ Driver's License ☐ Passport ☐ Other ID ISSUED ___ SIGNATURE _____ (after oath / affirmation) PHONE C / H / W ___ / ___ **or** ☐ MISC #___ AGENCY ___ EXPIRES ___ ❶
CW #2	#2 WITNESS's NAME _____ ☐ P/Known ☐ Non-Public ADDRESS _____ ☐ Driver's License ☐ Passport ☐ Other ID ISSUED ___ SIGNATURE _____ (after oath / affirmation) PHONE C / H / W ___ / ___ **or** ☐ MISC #___ AGENCY ___ EXPIRES ___ ❷

58 Fingerprint R T I M R P L

COMMISSION #:

Entry 59

59

Fingerprint

R
T
I
M
R
P
L

| SERVICE | DATE ____-____-20____ | TIME ____:____ am pm | ADDRESS | ☐ Office | NOTES | ☐ Stop | MILES | ☐ Notary $ | ☐ Adv. Travel $ | ☐ Rush $ | ☐ Copy $ | ☐ Other $ | TOTAL FEES $ |

SERVICE
TYPE ☐ Acknowledgment ☐ Jurat ☐ Signature Witnessing ☐ Copy Certification ☐ Oath/Affirmation ☐ Protest ☐ Other

DOCUMENT
DOC TYPE ☐ Deed G/QC/W ☐ DOT/Mortgage ☐ Trust Rev/Irrev/Cert ☐ Will ☐ POAF G/L D/S ☐ POAH/AHCD ☐ Affidavit ☐ Other
DOC DATE J F M A M J J A S O N D , DOC TITLE or TYPE
OF PAGES ☐ Inspect/Copy Request   Entry X-Ref

SIGNER
SATISFACTORY EVIDENCE ☐ Driver's License / Passport / Other ID *or* ☐ Credible Witness(es) *OR* ☐ Personal Knowledge
SIGNER's NAME
☐ For ☐ Non-Public   ADDRESS
PHONE C / H / W ___/___   *or* ☐ MISC
☐ Driver's License ☐ Passport ☐ Other ID # ___   ISSUED   AGENCY   EXPIRES
SIGNATURE ☐ (oath/affirmation, if any) ☐ (by Mark)

CW #1
#1 WITNESS's NAME
☐ P/Known ☐ Non-Public   ADDRESS
PHONE C / H / W ___/___   *or* ☐ MISC
☐ Driver's License ☐ Passport ☐ Other ID # ___   ISSUED   AGENCY   EXPIRES
❶ SIGNATURE ☐ (after oath / affirmation)

CW #2
#2 WITNESS's NAME
☐ P/Known ☐ Non-Public   ADDRESS
PHONE C / H / W ___/___   *or* ☐ MISC
☐ Driver's License ☐ Passport ☐ Other ID # ___   ISSUED   AGENCY   EXPIRES
❷ SIGNATURE ☐ (after oath / affirmation)

Entry 60

60

Fingerprint

R
T
I
M
R
P
L

| SERVICE | DATE ____-____-20____ | TIME ____:____ am pm | ADDRESS | ☐ Office | NOTES | ☐ Stop | MILES | ☐ Notary $ | ☐ Adv. Travel $ | ☐ Rush $ | ☐ Copy $ | ☐ Other $ | TOTAL FEES $ |

SERVICE
TYPE ☐ Acknowledgment ☐ Jurat ☐ Signature Witnessing ☐ Copy Certification ☐ Oath/Affirmation ☐ Protest ☐ Other

DOCUMENT
DOC TYPE ☐ Deed G/QC/W ☐ DOT/Mortgage ☐ Trust Rev/Irrev/Cert ☐ Will ☐ POAF G/L D/S ☐ POAH/AHCD ☐ Affidavit ☐ Other
DOC DATE J F M A M J J A S O N D , DOC TITLE or TYPE
OF PAGES ☐ Inspect/Copy Request   Entry X-Ref

SIGNER
SATISFACTORY EVIDENCE ☐ Driver's License / Passport / Other ID *or* ☐ Credible Witness(es) *OR* ☐ Personal Knowledge
SIGNER's NAME
☐ For ☐ Non-Public   ADDRESS
PHONE C / H / W ___/___   *or* ☐ MISC
☐ Driver's License ☐ Passport ☐ Other ID # ___   ISSUED   AGENCY   EXPIRES
SIGNATURE ☐ (oath/affirmation, if any) ☐ (by Mark)

CW #1
#1 WITNESS's NAME
☐ P/Known ☐ Non-Public   ADDRESS
PHONE C / H / W ___/___   *or* ☐ MISC
☐ Driver's License ☐ Passport ☐ Other ID # ___   ISSUED   AGENCY   EXPIRES
❶ SIGNATURE ☐ (after oath / affirmation)

CW #2
#2 WITNESS's NAME
☐ P/Known ☐ Non-Public   ADDRESS
PHONE C / H / W ___/___   *or* ☐ MISC
☐ Driver's License ☐ Passport ☐ Other ID # ___   ISSUED   AGENCY   EXPIRES
❷ SIGNATURE ☐ (after oath / affirmation)

NOTARY NAME (printed):

COMMISSION #:

Entry 61

☐ Office

SERVICE

DATE ___ - ___ -20___ | TIME ___:___ ☐ am ☐ pm | ADDRESS

☐ Stop ☐ MILES $___ | ☐ Notary $___ | ☐ Adv. Travel $___ | ☐ Rush $___ | ☐ Copy $___ | ☐ Other $___ | TOTAL FEES $___

NOTES

TYPE ☐ Acknowledgment ☐ Jurat ☐ Signature Witnessing ☐ Copy Certification ☐ Oath/Affirmation ☐ Other

DOCUMENT

DOC TYPE ☐ Deed G/QC/W ☐ DOT/Mortgage ☐ Trust Rev/Irrev/Cert ☐ Will ☐ POAF G/L D/S ☐ POAH/AHCD ☐ Affidavit ☐ Other

DOC DATE ___ - ___ - J F M A M J J A S O N D , ___

DOC TITLE or TYPE

☐ # OF PAGES ___ ☐ Inspect/Copy Request — Entry X-Ref #

SIGNER

☐ SATISFACTORY EVIDENCE ☐ Driver's License / Passport / Other ID *or* ☐ Credible Witness(es) *OR* ☐ Personal Knowledge

SIGNER's NAME ___ ☐ For ___ ☐ P/Known ___ | ☐ Driver's License ☐ Passport ☐ Non-Public ☐ Other ID | SIGNATURE ☐ (oath/affirmation, if any) ☐ (by Mark)

ADDRESS ___ ISSUED ___ EXPIRES ___

PHONE C / H / W ___ / ___ *or* ☐ MISC | # ___ AGENCY ___

Fingerprint R — R T I M R P L

CW #1

#1 WITNESS's NAME ___ ☐ P/Known ___ | ☐ Driver's License ☐ Passport ☐ Non-Public ☐ Other ID | SIGNATURE ☐ (after oath / affirmation)

ADDRESS ___ ISSUED ___ EXPIRES ___

PHONE C / H / W ___ / ___ *or* ☐ MISC | # ___ AGENCY ___ ❶

CW #2

#2 WITNESS's NAME ___ ☐ P/Known ___ | ☐ Driver's License ☐ Passport ☐ Non-Public ☐ Other ID | SIGNATURE ☐ (after oath / affirmation)

ADDRESS ___ ISSUED ___ EXPIRES ___

PHONE C / H / W ___ / ___ *or* ☐ MISC | # ___ AGENCY ___ ❷

Entry 62

☐ Office

SERVICE

DATE ___ - ___ -20___ | TIME ___:___ ☐ am ☐ pm | ADDRESS

☐ Stop ☐ MILES $___ | ☐ Notary $___ | ☐ Adv. Travel $___ | ☐ Rush $___ | ☐ Copy $___ | ☐ Other $___ | TOTAL FEES $___

NOTES

TYPE ☐ Acknowledgment ☐ Jurat ☐ Signature Witnessing ☐ Copy Certification ☐ Oath/Affirmation ☐ Other

DOCUMENT

DOC TYPE ☐ Deed G/QC/W ☐ DOT/Mortgage ☐ Trust Rev/Irrev/Cert ☐ Will ☐ POAF G/L D/S ☐ POAH/AHCD ☐ Affidavit ☐ Other

DOC DATE ___ - ___ - J F M A M J J A S O N D , ___

DOC TITLE or TYPE

☐ # OF PAGES ___ ☐ Inspect/Copy Request — Entry X-Ref #

SIGNER

☐ SATISFACTORY EVIDENCE ☐ Driver's License / Passport / Other ID *or* ☐ Credible Witness(es) *OR* ☐ Personal Knowledge

SIGNER's NAME ___ ☐ For ___ ☐ P/Known ___ | ☐ Driver's License ☐ Passport ☐ Non-Public ☐ Other ID | SIGNATURE ☐ (oath/affirmation, if any) ☐ (by Mark)

ADDRESS ___ ISSUED ___ EXPIRES ___

PHONE C / H / W ___ / ___ *or* ☐ MISC | # ___ AGENCY ___

Fingerprint R — R T I M R P L

CW #1

#1 WITNESS's NAME ___ ☐ P/Known ___ | ☐ Driver's License ☐ Passport ☐ Non-Public ☐ Other ID | SIGNATURE ☐ (after oath / affirmation)

ADDRESS ___ ISSUED ___ EXPIRES ___

PHONE C / H / W ___ / ___ *or* ☐ MISC | # ___ AGENCY ___ ❶

CW #2

#2 WITNESS's NAME ___ ☐ P/Known ___ | ☐ Driver's License ☐ Passport ☐ Non-Public ☐ Other ID | SIGNATURE ☐ (after oath / affirmation)

ADDRESS ___ ISSUED ___ EXPIRES ___

PHONE C / H / W ___ / ___ *or* ☐ MISC | # ___ AGENCY ___ ❷

Entry 63

NOTARY NAME (printed): _____ COMMISSION #: _____

63

| SERVICE | DATE ___ - ___ -20 ___ | TIME ___ : ___ ☐ am ☐ pm | ADDRESS | ☐ Office | NOTES | ☐ Stop | MILES | ☐ Notary $ | ☐ Adv. Travel $ | ☐ Rush $ | ☐ Copy $ | ☐ Other $ | TOTAL FEES $ |

Fingerprint

R
T
I
M
R
P
L

DOCUMENT

TYPE: ☐ Acknowledgment ☐ Jurat ☐ Signature Witnessing ☐ Copy Certification ☐ Oath/Affirmation ☐ Oath of Office ☐ Protest ☐ Other

DOC TYPE: ☐ Deed G/QC/W ☐ DOT/Mortgage ☐ Trust Rev/Irrev/Cert ☐ Will ☐ POAF G/L D/S ☐ POAH/AHCD ☐ Affidavit ☐ Other

DOC DATE J F M A M J / J A S O N D , ____ DOC TITLE or TYPE ____ # OF PAGES ____ ☐ Inspect/Copy Request Entry X-Ref # ____

SIGNER

☐ **SATISFACTORY EVIDENCE** ☐ Driver's License / Passport / Other ID *or* ☐ Credible Witness(es) **OR** ☐ Personal Knowledge

SIGNER's NAME ____ ☐ For ADDRESS ☐ Non-Public ☐ Driver's License ☐ Passport ☐ Other ID ISSUED SIGNATURE ☐ (oath/affirmation, if any)

PHONE C / H / W ___ / ___ *or* ☐ MISC # ____ AGENCY ____ EXPIRES

CW #1

#1 WITNESS's NAME ____ ☐ P/Known ADDRESS ☐ Non-Public ☐ Driver's License ☐ Passport ☐ Other ID ISSUED SIGNATURE ☐ (after oath / affirmation) ❶

PHONE C / H / W ___ / ___ *or* ☐ MISC # ____ AGENCY ____ EXPIRES

CW #2

#2 WITNESS's NAME ____ ☐ P/Known ADDRESS ☐ Non-Public ☐ Driver's License ☐ Passport ☐ Other ID ISSUED SIGNATURE ☐ (after oath / affirmation) ❷

PHONE C / H / W ___ / ___ *or* ☐ MISC # ____ AGENCY ____ EXPIRES

☐ (by Mark)

Entry 64

64

| SERVICE | DATE ___ - ___ -20 ___ | TIME ___ : ___ ☐ am ☐ pm | ADDRESS | ☐ Office | NOTES | ☐ Stop | MILES | ☐ Notary $ | ☐ Adv. Travel $ | ☐ Rush $ | ☐ Copy $ | ☐ Other $ | TOTAL FEES $ |

Fingerprint

R
T
I
M
R
P
L

DOCUMENT

TYPE: ☐ Acknowledgment ☐ Jurat ☐ Signature Witnessing ☐ Copy Certification ☐ Oath/Affirmation ☐ Oath of Office ☐ Protest ☐ Other

DOC TYPE: ☐ Deed G/QC/W ☐ DOT/Mortgage ☐ Trust Rev/Irrev/Cert ☐ Will ☐ POAF G/L D/S ☐ POAH/AHCD ☐ Affidavit ☐ Other

DOC DATE J F M A M J / J A S O N D , ____ DOC TITLE or TYPE ____ # OF PAGES ____ ☐ Inspect/Copy Request Entry X-Ref # ____

SIGNER

☐ **SATISFACTORY EVIDENCE** ☐ Driver's License / Passport / Other ID *or* ☐ Credible Witness(es) **OR** ☐ Personal Knowledge

SIGNER's NAME ____ ☐ For ADDRESS ☐ Non-Public ☐ Driver's License ☐ Passport ☐ Other ID ISSUED SIGNATURE ☐ (oath/affirmation, if any)

PHONE C / H / W ___ / ___ *or* ☐ MISC # ____ AGENCY ____ EXPIRES

CW #1

#1 WITNESS's NAME ____ ☐ P/Known ADDRESS ☐ Non-Public ☐ Driver's License ☐ Passport ☐ Other ID ISSUED SIGNATURE ☐ (after oath / affirmation) ❶

PHONE C / H / W ___ / ___ *or* ☐ MISC # ____ AGENCY ____ EXPIRES

CW #2

#2 WITNESS's NAME ____ ☐ P/Known ADDRESS ☐ Non-Public ☐ Driver's License ☐ Passport ☐ Other ID ISSUED SIGNATURE ☐ (after oath / affirmation) ❷

PHONE C / H / W ___ / ___ *or* ☐ MISC # ____ AGENCY ____ EXPIRES

☐ (by Mark)

NOTARY NAME (printed): _____

COMMISSION #: _____

Entry 65

65

☐ Office NOTES

DATE ___ - ___ -20___ TIME ___:___ ☐ am ☐ pm ADDRESS

☐ Stop MILES $___ ☐ Notary $___ ☐ Adv. Travel $___ ☐ Rush $___ ☐ Copy $___ ☐ Other $___ TOTAL FEES $___

Fingerprint

R
T
I
M
R
P
L

SERVICE — TYPE ☐ Acknowledgment ☐ Jurat ☐ Signature Witnessing ☐ Copy Certification ☐ Oath/Affirmation ☐ Oath of Office ☐ Protest ☐ Other

DOCUMENT — DOC TYPE ☐ Deed G/QC/W ☐ DOT/Mortgage ☐ Trust Rev/Irrev/Cert ☐ Will ☐ POAF G/L D/S ☐ POAH/AHCD ☐ Affidavit ☐ Other

DOC DATE J F M A M J J A S O N D ___ - ___ - ___

OF PAGES ___ ☐ Inspect/Copy Request

Entry X-Ref # ___

DOC TITLE or TYPE

SATISFACTORY EVIDENCE ☐ Driver's License / Passport / Other ID *or* ☐ Credible Witness(es) *OR* ☐ Personal Knowledge

SIGNER — SIGNER's NAME
☐ For ☐ Non-Public ADDRESS
☐ Driver's License ☐ Passport ☐ Other ID ISSUED SIGNATURE ☐ (oath/affirmation, if any)
PHONE C / H / W ___ / ___ *or* ☐ MISC # ___ AGENCY ___ EXPIRES

CW #1 — #1 WITNESS's NAME
☐ P/Known ADDRESS
☐ Driver's License ☐ Passport ☐ Other ID ISSUED SIGNATURE ☐ (after oath / affirmation) ❶
PHONE C / H / W ___ / ___ *or* ☐ MISC # ___ AGENCY ___ EXPIRES

CW #2 — #2 WITNESS's NAME
☐ P/Known ADDRESS
☐ Driver's License ☐ Passport ☐ Other ID ISSUED SIGNATURE ☐ (after oath / affirmation) ❷
PHONE C / H / W ___ / ___ *or* ☐ MISC # ___ AGENCY ___ EXPIRES

☐ (by Mark)

Entry 66

66

☐ Office NOTES

DATE ___ - ___ -20___ TIME ___:___ ☐ am ☐ pm ADDRESS

☐ Stop MILES $___ ☐ Notary $___ ☐ Adv. Travel $___ ☐ Rush $___ ☐ Copy $___ ☐ Other $___ TOTAL FEES $___

Fingerprint

R
T
I
M
R
P
L

SERVICE — TYPE ☐ Acknowledgment ☐ Jurat ☐ Signature Witnessing ☐ Copy Certification ☐ Oath/Affirmation ☐ Oath of Office ☐ Protest ☐ Other

DOCUMENT — DOC TYPE ☐ Deed G/QC/W ☐ DOT/Mortgage ☐ Trust Rev/Irrev/Cert ☐ Will ☐ POAF G/L D/S ☐ POAH/AHCD ☐ Affidavit ☐ Other

DOC DATE J F M A M J J A S O N D ___ - ___ - ___

OF PAGES ___ ☐ Inspect/Copy Request

Entry X-Ref # ___

DOC TITLE or TYPE

SATISFACTORY EVIDENCE ☐ Driver's License / Passport / Other ID *or* ☐ Credible Witness(es) *OR* ☐ Personal Knowledge

SIGNER — SIGNER's NAME
☐ For ☐ Non-Public ADDRESS
☐ Driver's License ☐ Passport ☐ Other ID ISSUED SIGNATURE ☐ (oath/affirmation, if any)
PHONE C / H / W ___ / ___ *or* ☐ MISC # ___ AGENCY ___ EXPIRES

CW #1 — #1 WITNESS's NAME
☐ P/Known ADDRESS
☐ Driver's License ☐ Passport ☐ Other ID ISSUED SIGNATURE ☐ (after oath / affirmation) ❶
PHONE C / H / W ___ / ___ *or* ☐ MISC # ___ AGENCY ___ EXPIRES

CW #2 — #2 WITNESS's NAME
☐ P/Known ADDRESS
☐ Driver's License ☐ Passport ☐ Other ID ISSUED SIGNATURE ☐ (after oath / affirmation) ❷
PHONE C / H / W ___ / ___ *or* ☐ MISC # ___ AGENCY ___ EXPIRES

☐ (by Mark)

NOTARY NAME (printed): _____

COMMISSION #: _____

Entry 67

SERVICE
- DATE ___ - ___ -20___ TIME ___ : ___ ☐ am ☐ pm
- ADDRESS
- ☐ Office NOTES
- ☐ Stop ☐ MILES ☐ Adv. Travel ☐ Rush ☐ Copy ☐ Other TOTAL FEES
- MILES $___ Notary $___ Adv. Travel $___ Rush $___ Copy $___ Other $___ $___

Fingerprint
R _____ T I M R P L

TYPE ☐ Acknowledgment ☐ Jurat ☐ Signature Witnessing ☐ Copy Certification ☐ Oath/Affirmation ☐ Protest ☐ Other

DOCUMENT
- DOC TYPE ☐ Deed G/QC/W ☐ DOT/Mortgage ☐ Trust Rev/Irrev/Cert ☐ Will ☐ POAF G/L D/S ☐ POAH/AHCD ☐ Affidavit ☐ Other
- DOC DATE J F M A M J J A S O N D , ___
- DOC TITLE or TYPE
- # OF PAGES ☐ Inspect/Copy Request Entry X-Ref #

SIGNER
- **SATISFACTORY EVIDENCE** ☐ Driver's License / Passport / Other ID *or* ☐ Credible Witness(es) **OR** ☐ Personal Knowledge
- SIGNER's NAME
- ☐ For ☐ Non-Public ☐ Driver's License ☐ Passport ☐ Other ID ISSUED _____ EXPIRES
- *or* ☐ MISC # _____ AGENCY
- PHONE C / H / W ___ / ___
- SIGNATURE ☐ (oath/affirmation, if any) ☐ (by Mark)

CW #1
- #1 WITNESS's NAME
- ☐ P/Known ☐ Non-Public ☐ Driver's License ☐ Passport ☐ Other ID ISSUED _____ EXPIRES
- *or* ☐ MISC # _____ AGENCY
- PHONE C / H / W ___ / ___
- SIGNATURE ☐ (after oath / affirmation) ❶

CW #2
- #2 WITNESS's NAME
- ☐ P/Known ☐ Non-Public ☐ Driver's License ☐ Passport ☐ Other ID ISSUED _____ EXPIRES
- *or* ☐ MISC # _____ AGENCY
- PHONE C / H / W ___ / ___
- SIGNATURE ☐ (after oath / affirmation) ❷

Entry 68

SERVICE
- DATE ___ - ___ -20___ TIME ___ : ___ ☐ am ☐ pm
- ADDRESS
- ☐ Office NOTES
- ☐ Stop ☐ MILES ☐ Adv. Travel ☐ Rush ☐ Copy ☐ Other TOTAL FEES
- MILES $___ Notary $___ Adv. Travel $___ Rush $___ Copy $___ Other $___ $___

Fingerprint
R _____ T I M R P L

TYPE ☐ Acknowledgment ☐ Jurat ☐ Signature Witnessing ☐ Copy Certification ☐ Oath/Affirmation ☐ Protest ☐ Other

DOCUMENT
- DOC TYPE ☐ Deed G/QC/W ☐ DOT/Mortgage ☐ Trust Rev/Irrev/Cert ☐ Will ☐ POAF G/L D/S ☐ POAH/AHCD ☐ Affidavit ☐ Other
- DOC DATE J F M A M J J A S O N D , ___
- DOC TITLE or TYPE
- # OF PAGES ☐ Inspect/Copy Request Entry X-Ref #

SIGNER
- **SATISFACTORY EVIDENCE** ☐ Driver's License / Passport / Other ID *or* ☐ Credible Witness(es) **OR** ☐ Personal Knowledge
- SIGNER's NAME
- ☐ For ☐ Non-Public ☐ Driver's License ☐ Passport ☐ Other ID ISSUED _____ EXPIRES
- *or* ☐ MISC # _____ AGENCY
- PHONE C / H / W ___ / ___
- SIGNATURE ☐ (oath/affirmation, if any) ☐ (by Mark)

CW #1
- #1 WITNESS's NAME
- ☐ P/Known ☐ Non-Public ☐ Driver's License ☐ Passport ☐ Other ID ISSUED _____ EXPIRES
- *or* ☐ MISC # _____ AGENCY
- PHONE C / H / W ___ / ___
- SIGNATURE ☐ (after oath / affirmation) ❶

CW #2
- #2 WITNESS's NAME
- ☐ P/Known ☐ Non-Public ☐ Driver's License ☐ Passport ☐ Other ID ISSUED _____ EXPIRES
- *or* ☐ MISC # _____ AGENCY
- PHONE C / H / W ___ / ___
- SIGNATURE ☐ (after oath / affirmation) ❷

NOTARY NAME (printed):

Entry 69

69

Fingerprint

R
T
I
M
R
P
L

SERVICE
DATE — - -20
TIME : am pm

☐ Stop ☐ MILES ☐ Notary ☐ Adv. Travel ☐ Rush ☐ Copy ☐ Other TOTAL FEES
$ $ $ $ $ $ $

☐ Office NOTES ADDRESS

TYPE ☐ Acknowledgment ☐ Jurat ☐ Signature Witnessing ☐ Copy Certification ☐ Oath/Affirmation ☐ Oath of Office ☐ Protest ☐ Other

DOCUMENT
DOC TYPE ☐ Deed G/QC/W ☐ DOT/Mortgage ☐ Trust Rev/Irrev/Cert ☐ Will ☐ POAF G/L D/S ☐ POAH/AHCD ☐ Affidavit ☐ Other

DOC DATE J F M A M J J A S O N D ,
DOC TITLE or TYPE

OF PAGES ☐ Inspect/Copy Request Entry X-Ref

SIGNER
SATISFACTORY EVIDENCE ☐ Driver's License / Passport / Other ID *or* ☐ Credible Witness(es) *OR* ☐ Personal Knowledge

SIGNER's NAME
☐ For ☐ Non-Public ADDRESS
☐ Driver's License ☐ Passport ☐ Other ID ISSUED
or ☐ MISC
PHONE C / H / W / # AGENCY EXPIRES
SIGNATURE ☐ (oath/affirmation, if any)
⬆

CW #1
#1 WITNESS's NAME
☐ P/Known ☐ Non-Public ADDRESS
☐ Driver's License ☐ Passport ☐ Other ID ISSUED
or ☐ MISC
PHONE C / H / W / # AGENCY EXPIRES
SIGNATURE ☐ (after oath / affirmation)
❶

CW #2
#2 WITNESS's NAME
☐ P/Known ☐ Non-Public ADDRESS
☐ Driver's License ☐ Passport ☐ Other ID ISSUED
or ☐ MISC
PHONE C / H / W / # AGENCY EXPIRES
SIGNATURE ☐ (after oath / affirmation)
❷

☐ (by Mark)

Entry 70

70

Fingerprint

R
T
I
M
R
P
L

SERVICE
DATE — - -20
TIME : am pm

☐ Stop ☐ MILES ☐ Notary ☐ Adv. Travel ☐ Rush ☐ Copy ☐ Other TOTAL FEES
$ $ $ $ $ $ $

☐ Office NOTES ADDRESS

TYPE ☐ Acknowledgment ☐ Jurat ☐ Signature Witnessing ☐ Copy Certification ☐ Oath/Affirmation ☐ Oath of Office ☐ Protest ☐ Other

DOCUMENT
DOC TYPE ☐ Deed G/QC/W ☐ DOT/Mortgage ☐ Trust Rev/Irrev/Cert ☐ Will ☐ POAF G/L D/S ☐ POAH/AHCD ☐ Affidavit ☐ Other

DOC DATE J F M A M J J A S O N D ,
DOC TITLE or TYPE

OF PAGES ☐ Inspect/Copy Request Entry X-Ref

SIGNER
SATISFACTORY EVIDENCE ☐ Driver's License / Passport / Other ID *or* ☐ Credible Witness(es) *OR* ☐ Personal Knowledge

SIGNER's NAME
☐ For ☐ Non-Public ADDRESS
☐ Driver's License ☐ Passport ☐ Other ID ISSUED
or ☐ MISC
PHONE C / H / W / # AGENCY EXPIRES
SIGNATURE ☐ (oath/affirmation, if any)
⬆

CW #1
#1 WITNESS's NAME
☐ P/Known ☐ Non-Public ADDRESS
☐ Driver's License ☐ Passport ☐ Other ID ISSUED
or ☐ MISC
PHONE C / H / W / # AGENCY EXPIRES
SIGNATURE ☐ (after oath / affirmation)
❶

CW #2
#2 WITNESS's NAME
☐ P/Known ☐ Non-Public ADDRESS
☐ Driver's License ☐ Passport ☐ Other ID ISSUED
or ☐ MISC
PHONE C / H / W / # AGENCY EXPIRES
SIGNATURE ☐ (after oath / affirmation)
❷

☐ (by Mark)

NOTARY NAME (printed): _____

COMMISSION #: _____

Entry 71

SERVICE	☐ Stop	MILES	☐ Notary	☐ Adv. Travel	☐ Rush	☐ Copy	☐ Other	TOTAL FEES
			$	$	$	$	$	$

☐ Office NOTES

DATE ___ - ___ -20___   TIME ___ : ___ am pm   ADDRESS

Fingerprint

R
T
I
M
R
P
L

TYPE ☐ Acknowledgment ☐ Jurat ☐ Signature Witnessing ☐ Copy Certification ☐ Oath/Affirmation ☐ Oath of Office ☐ Protest ☐ Other

DOCUMENT

DOC TYPE ☐ Deed G/QC/W ☐ DOT/Mortgage ☐ Trust Rev/Irrev/Cert ☐ Will ☐ POAF G/L D/S ☐ POAH/AHCD ☐ Affidavit ☐ Other

DOC DATE ___ - ___ J F M A M J J A S O N D , ___   DOC TITLE or TYPE   # OF PAGES ___ ☐ Inspect/Copy Request   Entry X-Ref # ___

SIGNER

☐ SATISFACTORY EVIDENCE ☐ Driver's License / Passport / Other ID   *or*   ☐ Credible Witness(es)   **OR**   ☐ Personal Knowledge

SIGNER's NAME ___   ☐ For ☐ Non-Public   ADDRESS   ☐ Driver's License ☐ Passport ☐ Other ID   ISSUED   SIGNATURE ☐ (oath/affirmation, if any)   ☐ (by Mark)

PHONE C / H / W ___ / ___   *or* ☐ MISC   # ___   AGENCY ___   EXPIRES

CW #1

#1 WITNESS's NAME ___ ☐ P/Known   ADDRESS   ☐ Non-Public ☐ Driver's License ☐ Passport ☐ Other ID   ISSUED   SIGNATURE ☐ (after oath / affirmation)   ❶

PHONE C / H / W ___ / ___   *or* ☐ MISC   # ___   AGENCY ___   EXPIRES

CW #2

#2 WITNESS's NAME ___ ☐ P/Known   ADDRESS   ☐ Non-Public ☐ Driver's License ☐ Passport ☐ Other ID   ISSUED   SIGNATURE ☐ (after oath / affirmation)   ❷

PHONE C / H / W ___ / ___   *or* ☐ MISC   # ___   AGENCY ___   EXPIRES

Entry 72

SERVICE	☐ Stop	MILES	☐ Notary	☐ Adv. Travel	☐ Rush	☐ Copy	☐ Other	TOTAL FEES
			$	$	$	$	$	$

☐ Office NOTES

DATE ___ - ___ -20___   TIME ___ : ___ am pm   ADDRESS

Fingerprint

R
T
I
M
R
P
L

TYPE ☐ Acknowledgment ☐ Jurat ☐ Signature Witnessing ☐ Copy Certification ☐ Oath/Affirmation ☐ Oath of Office ☐ Protest ☐ Other

DOCUMENT

DOC TYPE ☐ Deed G/QC/W ☐ DOT/Mortgage ☐ Trust Rev/Irrev/Cert ☐ Will ☐ POAF G/L D/S ☐ POAH/AHCD ☐ Affidavit ☐ Other

DOC DATE ___ - ___ J F M A M J J A S O N D , ___   DOC TITLE or TYPE   # OF PAGES ___ ☐ Inspect/Copy Request   Entry X-Ref # ___

SIGNER

☐ SATISFACTORY EVIDENCE ☐ Driver's License / Passport / Other ID   *or*   ☐ Credible Witness(es)   **OR**   ☐ Personal Knowledge

SIGNER's NAME ___   ☐ For ☐ Non-Public   ADDRESS   ☐ Driver's License ☐ Passport ☐ Other ID   ISSUED   SIGNATURE ☐ (oath/affirmation, if any)   ☐ (by Mark)

PHONE C / H / W ___ / ___   *or* ☐ MISC   # ___   AGENCY ___   EXPIRES

CW #1

#1 WITNESS's NAME ___ ☐ P/Known   ADDRESS   ☐ Non-Public ☐ Driver's License ☐ Passport ☐ Other ID   ISSUED   SIGNATURE ☐ (after oath / affirmation)   ❶

PHONE C / H / W ___ / ___   *or* ☐ MISC   # ___   AGENCY ___   EXPIRES

CW #2

#2 WITNESS's NAME ___ ☐ P/Known   ADDRESS   ☐ Non-Public ☐ Driver's License ☐ Passport ☐ Other ID   ISSUED   SIGNATURE ☐ (after oath / affirmation)   ❷

PHONE C / H / W ___ / ___   *or* ☐ MISC   # ___   AGENCY ___   EXPIRES

NOTARY NAME (printed): _____

COMMISSION #: _____

Entry 73

73

Fingerprint

R

T
I
M
R
P

L

☐ Office

DATE ___ - ___ -20___ TIME ___:___ ☐ am ☐ pm ADDRESS _____

☐ Stop ☐ MILES ☐ Notary ☐ Adv. Travel ☐ Rush ☐ Copy ☐ Other TOTAL FEES
$ ___ $ ___ $ ___ $ ___ $ ___ $ ___

NOTES

SERVICE

TYPE ☐ Acknowledgment ☐ Jurat ☐ Signature Witnessing ☐ Copy Certification ☐ Oath/Affirmation ☐ Protest ☐ Other

DOCUMENT

DOC TYPE ☐ Deed G/QC/W ☐ DOT/Mortgage ☐ Trust Rev/Irrev/Cert ☐ Will ☐ POAF G/L D/S ☐ POAH/AHCD ☐ Affidavit ☐ Other

DOC DATE ___ - ___ - J F M A M J J A S O N D , ___ # OF PAGES ☐ Inspect/Copy Request Entry X-Ref #

DOC TITLE or TYPE _____

SATISFACTORY EVIDENCE ☐ Driver's License / Passport / Other ID *or* ☐ Credible Witness(es) **OR** ☐ Personal Knowledge

SIGNER

SIGNER's NAME _____

☐ For ☐ Non-Public ADDRESS _____

☐ Driver's License ☐ Passport ☐ Other ID ISSUED ___ EXPIRES ___

SIGNATURE ☐ (oath/affirmation, if any) ☐ (by Mark)

PHONE C / H / W ___ *or* ☐ MISC ___ # ___ AGENCY ___

↑

CW #1

#1 WITNESS's NAME _____

☐ P/Known ☐ Non-Public ADDRESS _____

☐ Driver's License ☐ Passport ☐ Other ID ISSUED ___ EXPIRES ___

SIGNATURE ☐ (after oath / affirmation)

PHONE C / H / W ___ *or* ☐ MISC ___ # ___ AGENCY ___

❶

CW #2

#2 WITNESS's NAME _____

☐ P/Known ☐ Non-Public ADDRESS _____

☐ Driver's License ☐ Passport ☐ Other ID ISSUED ___ EXPIRES ___

SIGNATURE ☐ (after oath / affirmation)

PHONE C / H / W ___ / ___ *or* ☐ MISC ___ # ___ AGENCY ___

❷

Entry 74

74

Fingerprint

R

T
I
M
R
P

L

☐ Office

DATE ___ - ___ -20___ TIME ___:___ ☐ am ☐ pm ADDRESS _____

☐ Stop ☐ MILES ☐ Notary ☐ Adv. Travel ☐ Rush ☐ Copy ☐ Other TOTAL FEES
$ ___ $ ___ $ ___ $ ___ $ ___ $ ___

NOTES

SERVICE

TYPE ☐ Acknowledgment ☐ Jurat ☐ Signature Witnessing ☐ Copy Certification ☐ Oath/Affirmation ☐ Protest ☐ Other

DOCUMENT

DOC TYPE ☐ Deed G/QC/W ☐ DOT/Mortgage ☐ Trust Rev/Irrev/Cert ☐ Will ☐ POAF G/L D/S ☐ POAH/AHCD ☐ Affidavit ☐ Other

DOC DATE ___ - ___ - J F M A M J J A S O N D , ___ # OF PAGES ☐ Inspect/Copy Request Entry X-Ref #

DOC TITLE or TYPE _____

SATISFACTORY EVIDENCE ☐ Driver's License / Passport / Other ID *or* ☐ Credible Witness(es) **OR** ☐ Personal Knowledge

SIGNER

SIGNER's NAME _____

☐ For ☐ Non-Public ADDRESS _____

☐ Driver's License ☐ Passport ☐ Other ID ISSUED ___ EXPIRES ___

SIGNATURE ☐ (oath/affirmation, if any) ☐ (by Mark)

PHONE C / H / W ___ *or* ☐ MISC ___ # ___ AGENCY ___

↑

CW #1

#1 WITNESS's NAME _____

☐ P/Known ☐ Non-Public ADDRESS _____

☐ Driver's License ☐ Passport ☐ Other ID ISSUED ___ EXPIRES ___

SIGNATURE ☐ (after oath / affirmation)

PHONE C / H / W ___ *or* ☐ MISC ___ # ___ AGENCY ___

❶

CW #2

#2 WITNESS's NAME _____

☐ P/Known ☐ Non-Public ADDRESS _____

☐ Driver's License ☐ Passport ☐ Other ID ISSUED ___ EXPIRES ___

SIGNATURE ☐ (after oath / affirmation)

PHONE C / H / W ___ / ___ *or* ☐ MISC ___ # ___ AGENCY ___

❷

NOTARY NAME (printed): _____

COMMISSION #: _____

Entry 75

SERVICE
- DATE ___ - ___ -20___ TIME ___:___ am/pm ADDRESS _____ □ Office NOTES
- □ Stop MILES $ Notary $ Adv. Travel $ Rush $ Copy $ Other TOTAL FEES $
- TYPE: □ Acknowledgment □ Jurat □ Signature Witnessing □ Copy Certification □ Oath/Affirmation □ Oath of Office □ Protest □ Other

DOCUMENT
- DOC TYPE: □ Deed G/QC/W □ DOT/Mortgage □ Trust Rev/Irrev/Cert □ Will □ POAF G/L D/S □ POAH/AHCD □ Affidavit □ Other
- DOC DATE: J F M A M J J A S O N D ,
- DOC TITLE or TYPE _____
- # OF PAGES ____ □ Inspect/Copy Request Entry X-Ref # ____

Fingerprint
R   L
T
I
M
R
P

SIGNER
- SATISFACTORY EVIDENCE □ Driver's License / Passport / Other ID *or* □ Credible Witness(es) **OR** □ Personal Knowledge
- SIGNER's NAME _____
- □ For ADDRESS _____
- PHONE C / H / W ___ / ___ □ Non-Public □ Driver's License □ Passport □ Other ID ISSUED ____ EXPIRES ____ #____ AGENCY ____ *or* □ MISC
- SIGNATURE □ (oath/affirmation, if any) □ (by Mark)
- ⬆

CW #1
- #1 WITNESS's NAME _____
- □ P/Known ADDRESS _____
- PHONE C / H / W ___ / ___ □ Non-Public □ Driver's License □ Passport □ Other ID ISSUED ____ EXPIRES ____ #____ AGENCY ____ *or* □ MISC
- SIGNATURE □ (after oath / affirmation)
- ❶

CW #2
- #2 WITNESS's NAME _____
- □ P/Known ADDRESS _____
- PHONE C / H / W ___ / ___ □ Non-Public □ Driver's License □ Passport □ Other ID ISSUED ____ EXPIRES ____ #____ AGENCY ____ *or* □ MISC
- SIGNATURE □ (after oath / affirmation)
- ❷

Entry 76

SERVICE
- DATE ___ - ___ -20___ TIME ___:___ am/pm ADDRESS _____ □ Office NOTES
- □ Stop MILES $ Notary $ Adv. Travel $ Rush $ Copy $ Other TOTAL FEES $
- TYPE: □ Acknowledgment □ Jurat □ Signature Witnessing □ Copy Certification □ Oath/Affirmation □ Oath of Office □ Protest □ Other

DOCUMENT
- DOC TYPE: □ Deed G/QC/W □ DOT/Mortgage □ Trust Rev/Irrev/Cert □ Will □ POAF G/L D/S □ POAH/AHCD □ Affidavit □ Other
- DOC DATE: J F M A M J J A S O N D ,
- DOC TITLE or TYPE _____
- # OF PAGES ____ □ Inspect/Copy Request Entry X-Ref # ____

Fingerprint
R   L
T
I
M
R
P

SIGNER
- SATISFACTORY EVIDENCE □ Driver's License / Passport / Other ID *or* □ Credible Witness(es) **OR** □ Personal Knowledge
- SIGNER's NAME _____
- □ For ADDRESS _____
- PHONE C / H / W ___ / ___ □ Non-Public □ Driver's License □ Passport □ Other ID ISSUED ____ EXPIRES ____ #____ AGENCY ____ *or* □ MISC
- SIGNATURE □ (oath/affirmation, if any) □ (by Mark)
- ⬆

CW #1
- #1 WITNESS's NAME _____
- □ P/Known ADDRESS _____
- PHONE C / H / W ___ / ___ □ Non-Public □ Driver's License □ Passport □ Other ID ISSUED ____ EXPIRES ____ #____ AGENCY ____ *or* □ MISC
- SIGNATURE □ (after oath / affirmation)
- ❶

CW #2
- #2 WITNESS's NAME _____
- □ P/Known ADDRESS _____
- PHONE C / H / W ___ / ___ □ Non-Public □ Driver's License □ Passport □ Other ID ISSUED ____ EXPIRES ____ #____ AGENCY ____ *or* □ MISC
- SIGNATURE □ (after oath / affirmation)
- ❷

COMMISSION #:

Entry 77

77

DATE - -20
TIME : am pm
☐ Stop MILES ☐ Notary ☐ Adv. Travel ☐ Rush ☐ Copy ☐ Other TOTAL FEES
$ $ $ $ $ $ $

☐ Office ADDRESS | NOTES

Fingerprint
R
T
I
M
R
P
L

SERVICE
TYPE ☐ Acknowledgment ☐ Jurat ☐ Signature Witnessing ☐ Copy Certification ☐ Oath/Affirmation ☐ Oath of Office ☐ Protest ☐ Other

DOCUMENT
DOC TYPE ☐ Deed G/QC/W ☐ DOT/Mortgage ☐ Trust Rev/Irrev/Cert ☐ Will ☐ POAF G/L D/S ☐ POAH/AHCD ☐ Affidavit ☐ Other
DOC DATE J F M A M J J A S O N D
DOC TITLE or TYPE
OF PAGES ☐ Inspect/Copy Request
Entry X-Ref #

SIGNER
☐ SATISFACTORY EVIDENCE ☐ Driver's License / Passport / Other ID *or* ☐ Credible Witness(es) *OR* ☐ Personal Knowledge
SIGNER's NAME
☐ For ADDRESS ☐ Non-Public ☐ Other ID ISSUED
PHONE C / H / W *or* ☐ MISC # AGENCY EXPIRES
SIGNATURE ☐ (oath/affirmation, if any)
☐ (by Mark)

CW #1
#1 WITNESS's NAME
☐ P/Known ADDRESS ☐ Non-Public ☐ Driver's License ☐ Passport ☐ Other ID ISSUED
PHONE C / H / W *or* ☐ MISC # AGENCY EXPIRES
SIGNATURE ☐ (after oath / affirmation) ❶

CW #2
#2 WITNESS's NAME
☐ P/Known ADDRESS ☐ Non-Public ☐ Driver's License ☐ Passport ☐ Other ID ISSUED
PHONE C / H / W *or* ☐ MISC # AGENCY EXPIRES
SIGNATURE ☐ (after oath / affirmation) ❷

Entry 78

78

DATE - -20
TIME : am pm
☐ Stop MILES ☐ Notary ☐ Adv. Travel ☐ Rush ☐ Copy ☐ Other TOTAL FEES
$ $ $ $ $ $ $

☐ Office ADDRESS | NOTES

Fingerprint
R
T
I
M
R
P
L

SERVICE
TYPE ☐ Acknowledgment ☐ Jurat ☐ Signature Witnessing ☐ Copy Certification ☐ Oath/Affirmation ☐ Oath of Office ☐ Protest ☐ Other

DOCUMENT
DOC TYPE ☐ Deed G/QC/W ☐ DOT/Mortgage ☐ Trust Rev/Irrev/Cert ☐ Will ☐ POAF G/L D/S ☐ POAH/AHCD ☐ Affidavit ☐ Other
DOC DATE J F M A M J J A S O N D
DOC TITLE or TYPE
OF PAGES ☐ Inspect/Copy Request
Entry X-Ref #

SIGNER
☐ SATISFACTORY EVIDENCE ☐ Driver's License / Passport / Other ID *or* ☐ Credible Witness(es) *OR* ☐ Personal Knowledge
SIGNER's NAME
☐ For ADDRESS ☐ Non-Public ☐ Other ID ISSUED
PHONE C / H / W *or* ☐ MISC # AGENCY EXPIRES
SIGNATURE ☐ (oath/affirmation, if any)
☐ (by Mark)

CW #1
#1 WITNESS's NAME
☐ P/Known ADDRESS ☐ Non-Public ☐ Driver's License ☐ Passport ☐ Other ID ISSUED
PHONE C / H / W *or* ☐ MISC # AGENCY EXPIRES
SIGNATURE ☐ (after oath / affirmation) ❶

CW #2
#2 WITNESS's NAME
☐ P/Known ADDRESS ☐ Non-Public ☐ Driver's License ☐ Passport ☐ Other ID ISSUED
PHONE C / H / W *or* ☐ MISC # AGENCY EXPIRES
SIGNATURE ☐ (after oath / affirmation) ❷

NOTARY NAME (printed): _____

COMMISSION #: _____

Entry 79

SERVICE

DATE ___ - ___ -20___ TIME ___ : ___ ☐ am ☐ pm
☐ Stop ☐ MILES ☐ Adv. Travel ☐ Rush ☐ Copy ☐ Other ☐ Office
TOTAL FEES
Notary $___ Adv.Travel $___ Rush $___ Copy $___ Other $___ $___
ADDRESS _____ NOTES _____

Fingerprint
R ☐ T ☐ I ☐ M ☐ R ☐ P
L

DOCUMENT

TYPE ☐ Acknowledgment ☐ Jurat ☐ Signature Witnessing ☐ Copy Certification ☐ Oath/Affirmation ☐ Protest ☐ Oath of Office ☐ Other
DOC TYPE ☐ Deed G/QC/W ☐ DOT/Mortgage ☐ Trust Rev/Irrev/Cert ☐ Will ☐ POAF G/L D/S ☐ POAH/AHCD ☐ Affidavit ☐ Other
DOC DATE J F M A M J J A S O N D
DOC TITLE or TYPE _____
OF PAGES ___ ☐ Inspect/Copy Request Entry X-Ref # ___

SIGNER

☐ SATISFACTORY EVIDENCE ☐ Driver's License / Passport / Other ID *or* ☐ Credible Witness(es) *OR* ☐ Personal Knowledge
SIGNER's NAME _____
☐ For ☐ MISC ☐ Non-Public ☐ Driver's License ☐ Passport ☐ Other ID ISSUED ___ EXPIRES ___
ADDRESS _____
PHONE C / H / W ___ / ___ #___ AGENCY ___
SIGNATURE ☐ (oath/affirmation, if any) ☐ (by Mark)

CW #1

#1 WITNESS's NAME _____
☐ P/Known ☐ MISC ☐ Non-Public ☐ Driver's License ☐ Passport ☐ Other ID ISSUED ___ EXPIRES ___
ADDRESS _____
PHONE C / H / W ___ / ___ #___ AGENCY ___
SIGNATURE ☐ (after oath / affirmation) ➊

CW #2

#2 WITNESS's NAME _____
☐ P/Known ☐ MISC ☐ Non-Public ☐ Driver's License ☐ Passport ☐ Other ID ISSUED ___ EXPIRES ___
ADDRESS _____
PHONE C / H / W ___ / ___ #___ AGENCY ___
SIGNATURE ☐ (after oath / affirmation) ➋

Entry 80

SERVICE

DATE ___ - ___ -20___ TIME ___ : ___ ☐ am ☐ pm
☐ Stop ☐ MILES ☐ Adv. Travel ☐ Rush ☐ Copy ☐ Other ☐ Office
TOTAL FEES
Notary $___ Adv.Travel $___ Rush $___ Copy $___ Other $___ $___
ADDRESS _____ NOTES _____

Fingerprint
R ☐ T ☐ I ☐ M ☐ R ☐ P
L

DOCUMENT

TYPE ☐ Acknowledgment ☐ Jurat ☐ Signature Witnessing ☐ Copy Certification ☐ Oath/Affirmation ☐ Protest ☐ Oath of Office ☐ Other
DOC TYPE ☐ Deed G/QC/W ☐ DOT/Mortgage ☐ Trust Rev/Irrev/Cert ☐ Will ☐ POAF G/L D/S ☐ POAH/AHCD ☐ Affidavit ☐ Other
DOC DATE J F M A M J J A S O N D
DOC TITLE or TYPE _____
OF PAGES ___ ☐ Inspect/Copy Request Entry X-Ref # ___

SIGNER

☐ SATISFACTORY EVIDENCE ☐ Driver's License / Passport / Other ID *or* ☐ Credible Witness(es) *OR* ☐ Personal Knowledge
SIGNER's NAME _____
☐ For ☐ MISC ☐ Non-Public ☐ Driver's License ☐ Passport ☐ Other ID ISSUED ___ EXPIRES ___
ADDRESS _____
PHONE C / H / W ___ / ___ #___ AGENCY ___
SIGNATURE ☐ (oath/affirmation, if any) ☐ (by Mark)

CW #1

#1 WITNESS's NAME _____
☐ P/Known ☐ MISC ☐ Non-Public ☐ Driver's License ☐ Passport ☐ Other ID ISSUED ___ EXPIRES ___
ADDRESS _____
PHONE C / H / W ___ / ___ #___ AGENCY ___
SIGNATURE ☐ (after oath / affirmation) ➊

CW #2

#2 WITNESS's NAME _____
☐ P/Known ☐ MISC ☐ Non-Public ☐ Driver's License ☐ Passport ☐ Other ID ISSUED ___ EXPIRES ___
ADDRESS _____
PHONE C / H / W ___ / ___ #___ AGENCY ___
SIGNATURE ☐ (after oath / affirmation) ➋

NOTARY NAME (printed): _____

COMMISSION #: _____

Entry 81

SERVICE

DATE ___-___-20___ TIME ___:___ ☐ am ☐ pm | ADDRESS | ☐ Office NOTES

☐ Stop ☐ MILES ☐ Notary ☐ Adv. Travel ☐ Rush ☐ Copy ☐ Other TOTAL FEES
$___ $___ $___ $___ $___ $___ $___

DOCUMENT

TYPE ☐ Acknowledgment ☐ Jurat ☐ Signature Witnessing ☐ Copy Certification ☐ Oath/Affirmation ☐ Oath of Office ☐ Protest ☐ Other

DOC TYPE ☐ Deed G/QC/W ☐ DOT/Mortgage ☐ Trust Rev/Irrev/Cert ☐ Will ☐ POAF G/L D/S ☐ POAH/AHCD ☐ Affidavit ☐ Other

DOC DATE J F M A M J / J A S O N D , ___ # OF PAGES ___ ☐ Inspect/Copy Request Entry X-Ref # ___

DOC TITLE or TYPE _____

SIGNER

☐ **SATISFACTORY EVIDENCE** ☐ Driver's License / Passport / Other ID *or* ☐ Credible Witness(es) *OR* ☐ Personal Knowledge

SIGNER's NAME _____ | ☐ Non-Public ☐ For ☐ Driver's License ☐ Passport ☐ Other ID ISSUED EXPIRES | ADDRESS

PHONE C / H / W ___/___ | # ___ *or* ☐ MISC AGENCY | SIGNATURE ☐ (oath/affirmation, if any)

CW #1

#1 WITNESS's NAME _____ | ☐ Non-Public ☐ P/Known ☐ Driver's License ☐ Passport ☐ Other ID ISSUED EXPIRES | ADDRESS

PHONE C / H / W ___/___ | # ___ *or* ☐ MISC AGENCY | SIGNATURE ☐ (after oath / affirmation) ❶

CW #2

#2 WITNESS's NAME _____ | ☐ Non-Public ☐ P/Known ☐ Driver's License ☐ Passport ☐ Other ID ISSUED EXPIRES | ADDRESS

PHONE C / H / W ___/___ | # ___ *or* ☐ MISC AGENCY | SIGNATURE ☐ (after oath / affirmation) ❷

Fingerprint
R T I M R P L

81

Entry 82

SERVICE

DATE ___-___-20___ TIME ___:___ ☐ am ☐ pm | ADDRESS | ☐ Office NOTES

☐ Stop ☐ MILES ☐ Notary ☐ Adv. Travel ☐ Rush ☐ Copy ☐ Other TOTAL FEES
$___ $___ $___ $___ $___ $___ $___

DOCUMENT

TYPE ☐ Acknowledgment ☐ Jurat ☐ Signature Witnessing ☐ Copy Certification ☐ Oath/Affirmation ☐ Oath of Office ☐ Protest ☐ Other

DOC TYPE ☐ Deed G/QC/W ☐ DOT/Mortgage ☐ Trust Rev/Irrev/Cert ☐ Will ☐ POAF G/L D/S ☐ POAH/AHCD ☐ Affidavit ☐ Other

DOC DATE J F M A M J / J A S O N D , ___ # OF PAGES ___ ☐ Inspect/Copy Request Entry X-Ref # ___

DOC TITLE or TYPE _____

SIGNER

☐ **SATISFACTORY EVIDENCE** ☐ Driver's License / Passport / Other ID *or* ☐ Credible Witness(es) *OR* ☐ Personal Knowledge

SIGNER's NAME _____ | ☐ Non-Public ☐ For ☐ Driver's License ☐ Passport ☐ Other ID ISSUED EXPIRES | ADDRESS

PHONE C / H / W ___/___ | # ___ *or* ☐ MISC AGENCY | SIGNATURE ☐ (oath/affirmation, if any)

CW #1

#1 WITNESS's NAME _____ | ☐ Non-Public ☐ P/Known ☐ Driver's License ☐ Passport ☐ Other ID ISSUED EXPIRES | ADDRESS

PHONE C / H / W ___/___ | # ___ *or* ☐ MISC AGENCY | SIGNATURE ☐ (after oath / affirmation) ❶

CW #2

#2 WITNESS's NAME _____ | ☐ Non-Public ☐ P/Known ☐ Driver's License ☐ Passport ☐ Other ID ISSUED EXPIRES | ADDRESS

PHONE C / H / W ___/___ | # ___ *or* ☐ MISC AGENCY | SIGNATURE ☐ (after oath / affirmation) ❷

Fingerprint
R T I M R P L

82

NOTARY NAME (printed):

COMMISSION #:

Entry 83

SERVICE
DATE ___ - ___ -20___ TIME ___:___ ☐ am ☐ pm ADDRESS ☐ Office NOTES
☐ Stop MILES ☐ Notary $ ☐ Adv. Travel $ ☐ Rush $ ☐ Copy $ ☐ Other $ TOTAL FEES $

DOCUMENT
TYPE ☐ Acknowledgment ☐ Jurat ☐ Signature Witnessing ☐ Copy Certification ☐ Oath/Affirmation ☐ Oath of Office ☐ Protest ☐ Other
DOC TYPE ☐ Deed G/QC/W ☐ DOT/Mortgage ☐ Trust Rev/Irrev/Cert ☐ Will ☐ POAF G/L D/S ☐ POAH/AHCD ☐ Affidavit ☐ Other
DOC DATE J F M A M J J A S O N D , ___ DOC TITLE or TYPE ___ # OF PAGES ☐ Inspect/Copy Request Entry X-Ref #

SIGNER
☐ SATISFACTORY EVIDENCE ☐ Driver's License / Passport / Other ID or ☐ Credible Witness(es) OR ☐ Personal Knowledge
SIGNER's NAME ___ ☐ For ☐ Non-Public ☐ Driver's License ☐ Passport ☐ Other ID ISSUED SIGNATURE ___ (oath/affirmation, if any) ☐ (by Mark)
ADDRESS ___
PHONE C / H / W ___ or ☐ MISC # ___ AGENCY ___ EXPIRES

CW #1
#1 WITNESS's NAME ___ ☐ P/Known ☐ Non-Public ☐ Driver's License ☐ Passport ☐ Other ID ISSUED SIGNATURE ___ (after oath / affirmation) ❶
ADDRESS ___
PHONE C / H / W ___ or ☐ MISC # ___ AGENCY ___ EXPIRES

CW #2
#2 WITNESS's NAME ___ ☐ P/Known ☐ Non-Public ☐ Driver's License ☐ Passport ☐ Other ID ISSUED SIGNATURE ___ (after oath / affirmation) ❷
ADDRESS ___
PHONE C / H / W ___ or ☐ MISC # ___ AGENCY ___ EXPIRES

Fingerprint
R
T
I
M
R
P
L

Entry 84

SERVICE
DATE ___ - ___ -20___ TIME ___:___ ☐ am ☐ pm ADDRESS ☐ Office NOTES
☐ Stop MILES ☐ Notary $ ☐ Adv. Travel $ ☐ Rush $ ☐ Copy $ ☐ Other $ TOTAL FEES $

DOCUMENT
TYPE ☐ Acknowledgment ☐ Jurat ☐ Signature Witnessing ☐ Copy Certification ☐ Oath/Affirmation ☐ Oath of Office ☐ Protest ☐ Other
DOC TYPE ☐ Deed G/QC/W ☐ DOT/Mortgage ☐ Trust Rev/Irrev/Cert ☐ Will ☐ POAF G/L D/S ☐ POAH/AHCD ☐ Affidavit ☐ Other
DOC DATE J F M A M J J A S O N D , ___ DOC TITLE or TYPE ___ # OF PAGES ☐ Inspect/Copy Request Entry X-Ref #

SIGNER
☐ SATISFACTORY EVIDENCE ☐ Driver's License / Passport / Other ID or ☐ Credible Witness(es) OR ☐ Personal Knowledge
SIGNER's NAME ___ ☐ For ☐ Non-Public ☐ Driver's License ☐ Passport ☐ Other ID ISSUED SIGNATURE ___ (oath/affirmation, if any) ☐ (by Mark)
ADDRESS ___
PHONE C / H / W ___ or ☐ MISC # ___ AGENCY ___ EXPIRES

CW #1
#1 WITNESS's NAME ___ ☐ P/Known ☐ Non-Public ☐ Driver's License ☐ Passport ☐ Other ID ISSUED SIGNATURE ___ (after oath / affirmation) ❶
ADDRESS ___
PHONE C / H / W ___ or ☐ MISC # ___ AGENCY ___ EXPIRES

CW #2
#2 WITNESS's NAME ___ ☐ P/Known ☐ Non-Public ☐ Driver's License ☐ Passport ☐ Other ID ISSUED SIGNATURE ___ (after oath / affirmation) ❷
ADDRESS ___
PHONE C / H / W ___ or ☐ MISC # ___ AGENCY ___ EXPIRES

Fingerprint
R
T
I
M
R
P
L

NOTARY NAME (printed): _____

COMMISSION #:

Entry 85

85

DATE __ - __ -20__	TIME __ : __ am/pm □ Office	ADDRESS	NOTES
□ Stop	MILES $	Notary $	Adv. Travel $	Rush $	Copy $	□ Other	TOTAL FEES $

Fingerprint

R
T
I
M
R
P
L

SERVICE
TYPE □ Acknowledgment □ Jurat □ Signature Witnessing □ Copy Certification □ Oath/Affirmation □ Oath of Office □ Protest □ Other

DOCUMENT
DOC TYPE □ Deed G/QC/W □ DOT/Mortgage □ Trust Rev/Irrev/Cert □ Will □ POAF G/L D/S □ POAH/AHCD □ Affidavit □ Other
DOC DATE J F M A M J J A S O N D , ____ DOC TITLE or TYPE ____ # OF PAGES ____ □ Inspect/Copy Request Entry X-Ref #

SIGNER
□ SATISFACTORY EVIDENCE □ Driver's License / Passport / Other ID *or* □ Credible Witness(es) *OR* □ Personal Knowledge
SIGNER's NAME ____ □ For ADDRESS ____
□ Driver's License □ Passport □ Non-Public □ Other ID ISSUED ____ SIGNATURE ____ □ (oath/affirmation, if any) □ (by Mark)
PHONE C/H/W __ / __ # ____ *or* □ MISC ____ AGENCY ____ EXPIRES ____

CW #1
#1 WITNESS's NAME ____ □ P/Known ADDRESS ____
□ Driver's License □ Passport □ Non-Public □ Other ID ISSUED ____ SIGNATURE ____ □ (after oath / affirmation) ❶
PHONE C/H/W __ / __ *or* □ MISC ____ # ____ AGENCY ____ EXPIRES ____

CW #2
#2 WITNESS's NAME ____ □ P/Known ADDRESS ____
□ Driver's License □ Passport □ Non-Public □ Other ID ISSUED ____ SIGNATURE ____ □ (after oath / affirmation) ❷
PHONE C/H/W __ / __ *or* □ MISC ____ # ____ AGENCY ____ EXPIRES ____

Entry 86

86

DATE __ - __ -20__	TIME __ : __ am/pm □ Office	ADDRESS	NOTES
□ Stop	MILES $	Notary $	Adv. Travel $	Rush $	Copy $	□ Other	TOTAL FEES $

Fingerprint

R
T
I
M
R
P
L

SERVICE
TYPE □ Acknowledgment □ Jurat □ Signature Witnessing □ Copy Certification □ Oath/Affirmation □ Oath of Office □ Protest □ Other

DOCUMENT
DOC TYPE □ Deed G/QC/W □ DOT/Mortgage □ Trust Rev/Irrev/Cert □ Will □ POAF G/L D/S □ POAH/AHCD □ Affidavit □ Other
DOC DATE J F M A M J J A S O N D , ____ DOC TITLE or TYPE ____ # OF PAGES ____ □ Inspect/Copy Request Entry X-Ref #

SIGNER
□ SATISFACTORY EVIDENCE □ Driver's License / Passport / Other ID *or* □ Credible Witness(es) *OR* □ Personal Knowledge
SIGNER's NAME ____ □ For ADDRESS ____
□ Driver's License □ Passport □ Non-Public □ Other ID ISSUED ____ SIGNATURE ____ □ (oath/affirmation, if any) □ (by Mark)
PHONE C/H/W __ / __ # ____ *or* □ MISC ____ AGENCY ____ EXPIRES ____

CW #1
#1 WITNESS's NAME ____ □ P/Known ADDRESS ____
□ Driver's License □ Passport □ Non-Public □ Other ID ISSUED ____ SIGNATURE ____ □ (after oath / affirmation) ❶
PHONE C/H/W __ / __ *or* □ MISC ____ # ____ AGENCY ____ EXPIRES ____

CW #2
#2 WITNESS's NAME ____ □ P/Known ADDRESS ____
□ Driver's License □ Passport □ Non-Public □ Other ID ISSUED ____ SIGNATURE ____ □ (after oath / affirmation) ❷
PHONE C/H/W __ / __ *or* □ MISC ____ # ____ AGENCY ____ EXPIRES ____

NOTARY NAME (printed): _____ COMMISSION #: _____

Entry 87

SERVICE | DATE __ - __ -20__ | TIME __ : __ am/pm | ADDRESS _____ | ☐ Office | NOTES
☐ Stop | MILES | ☐ Notary | ☐ Adv. Travel | ☐ Rush | ☐ Copy | ☐ Other | TOTAL FEES $
$ | $ | $ | $ | $ | $

DOCUMENT
TYPE: ☐ Acknowledgment ☐ Jurat ☐ Signature Witnessing ☐ Copy Certification ☐ Oath/Affirmation ☐ Oath of Office ☐ Protest ☐ Other
DOC TYPE: ☐ Deed G/QC/W ☐ DOT/Mortgage ☐ Trust Rev/Irrev/Cert ☐ Will ☐ POAF G/L D/S ☐ POAH/AHCD ☐ Affidavit ☐ Other
DOC DATE __ - __ J F M A M J J A S O N D , 20__   DOC TITLE or TYPE _____
OF PAGES ___ ☐ Inspect/Copy Request Entry X-Ref # ___

SIGNER
☐ SATISFACTORY EVIDENCE ☐ Driver's License / Passport / Other ID *or* ☐ Credible Witness(es) *OR* ☐ Personal Knowledge
SIGNER's NAME _____ | ☐ For ☐ Non-Public | ☐ Driver's License ☐ Passport ☐ Other ID ISSUED ___ SIGNATURE ☐ (oath/affirmation, if any) ☐ (by Mark)
PHONE C / H / W ___ | *or* ☐ MISC | # ___ AGENCY ___ EXPIRES ___

CW #1
#1 WITNESS's NAME ___ | ☐ P/Known ADDRESS ___ | ☐ Driver's License ☐ Passport ☐ Other ID ISSUED ___ SIGNATURE ☐ (after oath / affirmation) ❶
PHONE C / H / W ___ | *or* ☐ MISC | # ___ AGENCY ___ EXPIRES ___

CW #2
#2 WITNESS's NAME ___ | ☐ P/Known ADDRESS ___ | ☐ Driver's License ☐ Passport ☐ Other ID ISSUED ___ SIGNATURE ☐ (after oath / affirmation) ❷
PHONE C / H / W ___ | *or* ☐ MISC | # ___ AGENCY ___ EXPIRES ___

Fingerprint — R T I M R P L

Entry 88

SERVICE | DATE __ - __ -20__ | TIME __ : __ am/pm | ADDRESS _____ | ☐ Office | NOTES
☐ Stop | MILES | ☐ Notary | ☐ Adv. Travel | ☐ Rush | ☐ Copy | ☐ Other | TOTAL FEES $
$ | $ | $ | $ | $ | $

DOCUMENT
TYPE: ☐ Acknowledgment ☐ Jurat ☐ Signature Witnessing ☐ Copy Certification ☐ Oath/Affirmation ☐ Oath of Office ☐ Protest ☐ Other
DOC TYPE: ☐ Deed G/QC/W ☐ DOT/Mortgage ☐ Trust Rev/Irrev/Cert ☐ Will ☐ POAF G/L D/S ☐ POAH/AHCD ☐ Affidavit ☐ Other
DOC DATE __ - __ J F M A M J J A S O N D , 20__   DOC TITLE or TYPE _____
OF PAGES ___ ☐ Inspect/Copy Request Entry X-Ref # ___

SIGNER
☐ SATISFACTORY EVIDENCE ☐ Driver's License / Passport / Other ID *or* ☐ Credible Witness(es) *OR* ☐ Personal Knowledge
SIGNER's NAME _____ | ☐ For ☐ Non-Public | ☐ Driver's License ☐ Passport ☐ Other ID ISSUED ___ SIGNATURE ☐ (oath/affirmation, if any) ☐ (by Mark)
PHONE C / H / W ___ | *or* ☐ MISC | # ___ AGENCY ___ EXPIRES ___

CW #1
#1 WITNESS's NAME ___ | ☐ P/Known ADDRESS ___ | ☐ Driver's License ☐ Passport ☐ Other ID ISSUED ___ SIGNATURE ☐ (after oath / affirmation) ❶
PHONE C / H / W ___ | *or* ☐ MISC | # ___ AGENCY ___ EXPIRES ___

CW #2
#2 WITNESS's NAME ___ | ☐ P/Known ADDRESS ___ | ☐ Driver's License ☐ Passport ☐ Other ID ISSUED ___ SIGNATURE ☐ (after oath / affirmation) ❷
PHONE C / H / W ___ | *or* ☐ MISC | # ___ AGENCY ___ EXPIRES ___

Fingerprint — R T I M R P L

COMMISSION #:

NOTARY NAME (printed): _____

Entry 89

89 | Fingerprint

R
T
I
M
R
P
L

☐ Stop ☐ MILES ☐ Notary ☐ Adv. Travel ☐ Rush ☐ Copy ☐ Other   TOTAL FEES
$ $ $ $ $ $ $

☐ Office   NOTES

SERVICE
DATE ___ - ___ -20___   TIME ___ : ___ am/pm   ADDRESS
TYPE ☐ Acknowledgment ☐ Jurat ☐ Signature Witnessing ☐ Copy Certification ☐ Oath/Affirmation ☐ Oath of Office ☐ Protest ☐ Other

DOCUMENT
DOC TYPE ☐ Deed G/QC/W ☐ DOT/Mortgage ☐ Trust Rev/Irrev/Cert ☐ Will ☐ POAF G/L D/S ☐ POAH/AHCD ☐ Affidavit ☐ Other
DOC DATE J F M A M J J A S O N D , ___   DOC TITLE or TYPE   # OF PAGES ___ ☐ Inspect/Copy Request   Entry X-Ref #

SIGNER
☐ SATISFACTORY EVIDENCE ☐ Driver's License / Passport / Other ID *or* ☐ Credible Witness(es)   *OR*   ☐ Personal Knowledge
SIGNER's NAME   ☐ For ADDRESS   ☐ Non-Public ☐ Driver's License ☐ Passport ☐ Other ID   ISSUED   SIGNATURE ☐ (oath/affirmation, if any)
PHONE C / H / W ___ / ___   *or* ☐ MISC   # ___   AGENCY   EXPIRES

CW #1
#1 WITNESS's NAME   ☐ P/Known ADDRESS   ☐ Non-Public ☐ Driver's License ☐ Passport ☐ Other ID   ISSUED   SIGNATURE ☐ (after oath / affirmation) ❶
PHONE C / H / W ___ / ___   *or* ☐ MISC   # ___   AGENCY   EXPIRES

CW #2
#2 WITNESS's NAME   ☐ P/Known ADDRESS   ☐ Non-Public ☐ Driver's License ☐ Passport ☐ Other ID   ISSUED   SIGNATURE ☐ (after oath / affirmation) ❷
PHONE C / H / W ___ / ___   *or* ☐ MISC   # ___   AGENCY   EXPIRES

☐ (by Mark)

Entry 90

90 | Fingerprint

R
T
I
M
R
P
L

☐ Stop ☐ MILES ☐ Notary ☐ Adv. Travel ☐ Rush ☐ Copy ☐ Other   TOTAL FEES
$ $ $ $ $ $ $

☐ Office   NOTES

SERVICE
DATE ___ - ___ -20___   TIME ___ : ___ am/pm   ADDRESS
TYPE ☐ Acknowledgment ☐ Jurat ☐ Signature Witnessing ☐ Copy Certification ☐ Oath/Affirmation ☐ Oath of Office ☐ Protest ☐ Other

DOCUMENT
DOC TYPE ☐ Deed G/QC/W ☐ DOT/Mortgage ☐ Trust Rev/Irrev/Cert ☐ Will ☐ POAF G/L D/S ☐ POAH/AHCD ☐ Affidavit ☐ Other
DOC DATE J F M A M J J A S O N D , ___   DOC TITLE or TYPE   # OF PAGES ___ ☐ Inspect/Copy Request   Entry X-Ref #

SIGNER
☐ SATISFACTORY EVIDENCE ☐ Driver's License / Passport / Other ID *or* ☐ Credible Witness(es)   *OR*   ☐ Personal Knowledge
SIGNER's NAME   ☐ For ADDRESS   ☐ Non-Public ☐ Driver's License ☐ Passport ☐ Other ID   ISSUED   SIGNATURE ☐ (oath/affirmation, if any)
PHONE C / H / W ___ / ___   *or* ☐ MISC   # ___   AGENCY   EXPIRES

CW #1
#1 WITNESS's NAME   ☐ P/Known ADDRESS   ☐ Non-Public ☐ Driver's License ☐ Passport ☐ Other ID   ISSUED   SIGNATURE ☐ (after oath / affirmation) ❶
PHONE C / H / W ___ / ___   *or* ☐ MISC   # ___   AGENCY   EXPIRES

CW #2
#2 WITNESS's NAME   ☐ P/Known ADDRESS   ☐ Non-Public ☐ Driver's License ☐ Passport ☐ Other ID   ISSUED   SIGNATURE ☐ (after oath / affirmation) ❷
PHONE C / H / W ___ / ___   *or* ☐ MISC   # ___   AGENCY   EXPIRES

☐ (by Mark)

NOTARY NAME (printed): _____   COMMISSION #: _____

Entry 91

91 | Fingerprint

SERVICE	□ Stop MILES	□ Notary	□ Adv. Travel	□ Rush	□ Copy	□ Other TOTAL FEES
		$	$	$	$	$ $

DATE ___ - ___ -20___   TIME ___:___ □ am □ pm ADDRESS _____ □ Office NOTES _____

R
T
I
M
R
P
L

DOCUMENT
TYPE □ Acknowledgment □ Jurat □ Signature Witnessing □ Copy Certification □ Oath/Affirmation □ Oath of Office □ Protest □ Other
DOC TYPE □ Deed G/QC/W □ DOT/Mortgage □ Trust Rev/Irrev/Cert □ Will □ POAF G/L D/S □ POAH/AHCD □ Affidavit □ Other
DOC DATE ___ J F M A M J J A S O N D , ___   DOC TITLE or TYPE _____   # OF PAGES ___ □ Inspect/Copy Request Entry X-Ref # ___

SIGNER
□ SATISFACTORY EVIDENCE □ Driver's License / Passport / Other ID   *or* □ Credible Witness(es)   **OR**   □ Personal Knowledge
SIGNER's NAME _____ □ For □ Non-Public ADDRESS _____
□ Driver's License □ Passport □ Other ID ISSUED ___ SIGNATURE ___ □ (oath/affirmation, if any) □ (by Mark)
PHONE C / H / W ___ / ___ *or* □ MISC # ___ AGENCY ___ EXPIRES ___

CW #1
#1 WITNESS's NAME _____ □ P/Known □ Non-Public ADDRESS _____
□ Driver's License □ Passport □ Other ID ISSUED ___ SIGNATURE ___ □ (after oath / affirmation) ❶
PHONE C / H / W ___ / ___ *or* □ MISC # ___ AGENCY ___ EXPIRES ___

CW #2
#2 WITNESS's NAME _____ □ P/Known □ Non-Public ADDRESS _____
□ Driver's License □ Passport □ Other ID ISSUED ___ SIGNATURE ___ □ (after oath / affirmation) ❷
PHONE C / H / W ___ / ___ *or* □ MISC # ___ AGENCY ___ EXPIRES ___

Entry 92

92 | Fingerprint

SERVICE	□ Stop MILES	□ Notary	□ Adv. Travel	□ Rush	□ Copy	□ Other TOTAL FEES
		$	$	$	$	$ $

DATE ___ - ___ -20___   TIME ___:___ □ am □ pm ADDRESS _____ □ Office NOTES _____

R
T
I
M
R
P
L

DOCUMENT
TYPE □ Acknowledgment □ Jurat □ Signature Witnessing □ Copy Certification □ Oath/Affirmation □ Oath of Office □ Protest □ Other
DOC TYPE □ Deed G/QC/W □ DOT/Mortgage □ Trust Rev/Irrev/Cert □ Will □ POAF G/L D/S □ POAH/AHCD □ Affidavit □ Other
DOC DATE ___ J F M A M J J A S O N D , ___   DOC TITLE or TYPE _____   # OF PAGES ___ □ Inspect/Copy Request Entry X-Ref # ___

SIGNER
□ SATISFACTORY EVIDENCE □ Driver's License / Passport / Other ID   *or* □ Credible Witness(es)   **OR**   □ Personal Knowledge
SIGNER's NAME _____ □ For □ Non-Public ADDRESS _____
□ Driver's License □ Passport □ Other ID ISSUED ___ SIGNATURE ___ □ (oath/affirmation, if any) □ (by Mark)
PHONE C / H / W ___ / ___ *or* □ MISC # ___ AGENCY ___ EXPIRES ___

CW #1
#1 WITNESS's NAME _____ □ P/Known □ Non-Public ADDRESS _____
□ Driver's License □ Passport □ Other ID ISSUED ___ SIGNATURE ___ □ (after oath / affirmation) ❶
PHONE C / H / W ___ / ___ *or* □ MISC # ___ AGENCY ___ EXPIRES ___

CW #2
#2 WITNESS's NAME _____ □ P/Known □ Non-Public ADDRESS _____
□ Driver's License □ Passport □ Other ID ISSUED ___ SIGNATURE ___ □ (after oath / affirmation) ❷
PHONE C / H / W ___ / ___ *or* □ MISC # ___ AGENCY ___ EXPIRES ___

Entry 93

COMMISSION #: _____

NOTARY NAME (printed): _____

SERVICE	DATE __ - __ -20__ TIME __ : __ am / pm — ☐ Office ☐ Stop MILES ☐ Notary ☐ Adv. Travel ☐ Rush ☐ Copy ☐ Other TOTAL FEES — $ $ $ $ $ $ — NOTES — ADDRESS
	TYPE ☐ Acknowledgment ☐ Jurat ☐ Signature Witnessing ☐ Copy Certification ☐ Oath/Affirmation ☐ Oath of Office ☐ Protest ☐ Other
DOCUMENT	DOC TYPE ☐ Deed G/QC/W ☐ DOT/Mortgage ☐ Trust Rev/Irrev/Cert ☐ Will ☐ POAF G/L D/S ☐ POAH/AHCD ☐ Affidavit ☐ Other
	DOC DATE J F M A M J J A S O N D , ____ DOC TITLE or TYPE — # OF PAGES ☐ Inspect/Copy Request — Entry X-Ref #

Fingerprint R T I M R P L

SATISFACTORY EVIDENCE ☐ Driver's License / Passport / Other ID *or* ☐ Credible Witness(es) **OR** ☐ Personal Knowledge

SIGNER	SIGNER's NAME ☐ For ☐ Non-Public ☐ P/Known ADDRESS — ☐ Driver's License ☐ Passport ☐ Other ID ISSUED _____ EXPIRES _____ # _____ AGENCY _____ — *or* ☐ MISC — PHONE C / H / W ____ / ____ — SIGNATURE ☐ (oath/affirmation, if any) ☐ (by Mark) ⬆
CW #1	#1 WITNESS's NAME ☐ Non-Public ☐ P/Known ADDRESS — ☐ Driver's License ☐ Passport ☐ Other ID ISSUED _____ EXPIRES _____ # _____ AGENCY _____ — *or* ☐ MISC — PHONE C / H / W ____ / ____ — SIGNATURE ☐ (after oath / affirmation) ❶
CW #2	#2 WITNESS's NAME ☐ Non-Public ☐ P/Known ADDRESS — ☐ Driver's License ☐ Passport ☐ Other ID ISSUED _____ EXPIRES _____ # _____ AGENCY _____ — *or* ☐ MISC — PHONE C / H / W ____ / ____ — SIGNATURE ☐ (after oath / affirmation) ❷

93

Entry 94

SERVICE	DATE __ - __ -20__ TIME __ : __ am / pm — ☐ Office ☐ Stop MILES ☐ Notary ☐ Adv. Travel ☐ Rush ☐ Copy ☐ Other TOTAL FEES — $ $ $ $ $ $ — NOTES — ADDRESS
	TYPE ☐ Acknowledgment ☐ Jurat ☐ Signature Witnessing ☐ Copy Certification ☐ Oath/Affirmation ☐ Oath of Office ☐ Protest ☐ Other
DOCUMENT	DOC TYPE ☐ Deed G/QC/W ☐ DOT/Mortgage ☐ Trust Rev/Irrev/Cert ☐ Will ☐ POAF G/L D/S ☐ POAH/AHCD ☐ Affidavit ☐ Other
	DOC DATE J F M A M J J A S O N D , ____ DOC TITLE or TYPE — # OF PAGES ☐ Inspect/Copy Request — Entry X-Ref #

Fingerprint R T I M R P L

SATISFACTORY EVIDENCE ☐ Driver's License / Passport / Other ID *or* ☐ Credible Witness(es) **OR** ☐ Personal Knowledge

SIGNER	SIGNER's NAME ☐ For ☐ Non-Public ☐ P/Known ADDRESS — ☐ Driver's License ☐ Passport ☐ Other ID ISSUED _____ EXPIRES _____ # _____ AGENCY _____ — *or* ☐ MISC — PHONE C / H / W ____ / ____ — SIGNATURE ☐ (oath/affirmation, if any) ☐ (by Mark) ⬆
CW #1	#1 WITNESS's NAME ☐ Non-Public ☐ P/Known ADDRESS — ☐ Driver's License ☐ Passport ☐ Other ID ISSUED _____ EXPIRES _____ # _____ AGENCY _____ — *or* ☐ MISC — PHONE C / H / W ____ / ____ — SIGNATURE ☐ (after oath / affirmation) ❶
CW #2	#2 WITNESS's NAME ☐ Non-Public ☐ P/Known ADDRESS — ☐ Driver's License ☐ Passport ☐ Other ID ISSUED _____ EXPIRES _____ # _____ AGENCY _____ — *or* ☐ MISC — PHONE C / H / W ____ / ____ — SIGNATURE ☐ (after oath / affirmation) ❷

94

Entry 95

95	Fingerprint

SERVICE
DATE - -20 TIME : am / pm □ Office ADDRESS NOTES
□ Stop MILES □ Notary $ □ Adv. Travel $ □ Rush $ □ Copy $ □ Other $ TOTAL FEES $

Fingerprint — R T I M R P L

DOCUMENT
TYPE □ Acknowledgment □ Jurat □ Signature Witnessing □ Copy Certification □ Oath/Affirmation □ Oath of Office □ Protest □ Other
DOC TYPE □ Deed G/R/W □ DOT/Mortgage □ Trust Rev/Irrev/Cert □ Will □ POAF G/L D/S □ POAH/AHCD □ Affidavit □ Other
DOC DATE J F M A M J J A S O N D , DOC TITLE or TYPE □ # OF PAGES □ Inspect/Copy Request — Entry X-Ref #

SIGNER
□ SATISFACTORY EVIDENCE □ Driver's License / Passport / Other ID *or* □ Credible Witness(es) **OR** □ Personal Knowledge
SIGNER's NAME □ For □ Non-Public ADDRESS □ Driver's License □ Passport □ Other ID ISSUED SIGNATURE □ (oath/affirmation, if any) □ (by Mark)
PHONE C / H / W / *or* □ MISC # AGENCY EXPIRES

CW #1
#1 WITNESS's NAME □ P/Known □ Non-Public ADDRESS □ Driver's License □ Passport □ Other ID ISSUED SIGNATURE □ (after oath / affirmation)
PHONE C / H / W / *or* □ MISC # AGENCY EXPIRES ❶

CW #2
#2 WITNESS's NAME □ P/Known □ Non-Public ADDRESS □ Driver's License □ Passport □ Other ID ISSUED SIGNATURE □ (after oath / affirmation)
PHONE C / H / W / *or* □ MISC # AGENCY EXPIRES ❷

Entry 96

96	Fingerprint

SERVICE
DATE - -20 TIME : am / pm □ Office ADDRESS NOTES
□ Stop MILES □ Notary $ □ Adv. Travel $ □ Rush $ □ Copy $ □ Other $ TOTAL FEES $

Fingerprint — R T I M R P L

DOCUMENT
TYPE □ Acknowledgment □ Jurat □ Signature Witnessing □ Copy Certification □ Oath/Affirmation □ Oath of Office □ Protest □ Other
DOC TYPE □ Deed G/R/W □ DOT/Mortgage □ Trust Rev/Irrev/Cert □ Will □ POAF G/L D/S □ POAH/AHCD □ Affidavit □ Other
DOC DATE J F M A M J J A S O N D , DOC TITLE or TYPE □ # OF PAGES □ Inspect/Copy Request — Entry X-Ref #

SIGNER
□ SATISFACTORY EVIDENCE □ Driver's License / Passport / Other ID *or* □ Credible Witness(es) **OR** □ Personal Knowledge
SIGNER's NAME □ For □ Non-Public ADDRESS □ Driver's License □ Passport □ Other ID ISSUED SIGNATURE □ (oath/affirmation, if any) □ (by Mark)
PHONE C / H / W / *or* □ MISC # AGENCY EXPIRES

CW #1
#1 WITNESS's NAME □ P/Known □ Non-Public ADDRESS □ Driver's License □ Passport □ Other ID ISSUED SIGNATURE □ (after oath / affirmation)
PHONE C / H / W / *or* □ MISC # AGENCY EXPIRES ❶

CW #2
#2 WITNESS's NAME □ P/Known □ Non-Public ADDRESS □ Driver's License □ Passport □ Other ID ISSUED SIGNATURE □ (after oath / affirmation)
PHONE C / H / W / *or* □ MISC # AGENCY EXPIRES ❷

COMMISSION #: _____

NOTARY NAME (printed): _____

Entry 97

97

DATE ___ - ___ -20___ | TIME ___:___ □ am □ pm | ADDRESS | □ Office | NOTES

□ Stop □ MILES □ Notary □ Adv. Travel □ Rush □ Copy □ Other | TOTAL FEES
$___ $___ $___ $___ $___ $___ $___ $___

SERVICE
TYPE □ Acknowledgment □ Jurat □ Signature Witnessing □ Copy Certification □ Oath/Affirmation □ Oath of Office □ Protest □ Other

DOCUMENT
DOC TYPE □ Deed G/QC/W □ DOT/Mortgage □ Trust Rev/Irrev/Cert □ Will □ POAF G/L D/S □ POAH/AHCD □ Affidavit □ Other
DOC DATE J F M A M J J A S O N D , ___ DOC TITLE or TYPE | # OF PAGES □ Inspect/Copy Request Entry X-Ref #

Fingerprint
R
T
I
M
R
P
L

SIGNER
□ SATISFACTORY EVIDENCE □ Driver's License / Passport / Other ID *or* □ Credible Witness(es) *OR* □ Personal Knowledge
SIGNER's NAME | □ For ADDRESS | □ Non-Public | □ Driver's License □ Passport □ Other ID | ISSUED | EXPIRES | SIGNATURE □ (oath/affirmation, if any)
PHONE C / H / W | *or* □ MISC | # | AGENCY | ⬆

CW #1
#1 WITNESS's NAME | □ P/Known ADDRESS | □ Non-Public | □ Driver's License □ Passport □ Other ID | ISSUED | EXPIRES | SIGNATURE □ (after oath / affirmation)
PHONE C / H / W | *or* □ MISC | # | AGENCY | ❶

CW #2
#2 WITNESS's NAME | □ P/Known ADDRESS | □ Non-Public | □ Driver's License □ Passport □ Other ID | ISSUED | EXPIRES | SIGNATURE □ (after oath / affirmation)
PHONE C / H / W | *or* □ MISC | # | AGENCY | ❷

□ (by Mark)

Entry 98

98

DATE ___ - ___ -20___ | TIME ___:___ □ am □ pm | ADDRESS | □ Office | NOTES

□ Stop □ MILES □ Notary □ Adv. Travel □ Rush □ Copy □ Other | TOTAL FEES
$___ $___ $___ $___ $___ $___ $___ $___

SERVICE
TYPE □ Acknowledgment □ Jurat □ Signature Witnessing □ Copy Certification □ Oath/Affirmation □ Oath of Office □ Protest □ Other

DOCUMENT
DOC TYPE □ Deed G/QC/W □ DOT/Mortgage □ Trust Rev/Irrev/Cert □ Will □ POAF G/L D/S □ POAH/AHCD □ Affidavit □ Other
DOC DATE J F M A M J J A S O N D , ___ DOC TITLE or TYPE | # OF PAGES □ Inspect/Copy Request Entry X-Ref #

Fingerprint
R
T
I
M
R
P
L

SIGNER
□ SATISFACTORY EVIDENCE □ Driver's License / Passport / Other ID *or* □ Credible Witness(es) *OR* □ Personal Knowledge
SIGNER's NAME | □ For ADDRESS | □ Non-Public | □ Driver's License □ Passport □ Other ID | ISSUED | EXPIRES | SIGNATURE □ (oath/affirmation, if any)
PHONE C / H / W | *or* □ MISC | # | AGENCY | ⬆

CW #1
#1 WITNESS's NAME | □ P/Known ADDRESS | □ Non-Public | □ Driver's License □ Passport □ Other ID | ISSUED | EXPIRES | SIGNATURE □ (after oath / affirmation)
PHONE C / H / W | *or* □ MISC | # | AGENCY | ❶

CW #2
#2 WITNESS's NAME | □ P/Known ADDRESS | □ Non-Public | □ Driver's License □ Passport □ Other ID | ISSUED | EXPIRES | SIGNATURE □ (after oath / affirmation)
PHONE C / H / W | *or* □ MISC | # | AGENCY | ❷

□ (by Mark)

Entry 99

SERVICE		
DATE _ - _ -20_	TIME _ : _ ☐ am ☐ pm	☐ Stop ☐ Office
MILES	Adv. Travel $	Rush $	Notary $	Copy $	Other $	TOTAL FEES $

NOTES / ADDRESS

Fingerprint
R
T
I
M
R
P
L

TYPE ☐ Acknowledgment ☐ Jurat ☐ Signature Witnessing ☐ Copy Certification ☐ Oath/Affirmation ☐ Protest ☐ Other

DOCUMENT
DOC TYPE ☐ Deed G/QC/W ☐ DOT/Mortgage ☐ Trust Rev/Irrev/Cert ☐ Will ☐ POAF G/L D/S ☐ POAH/AHCD ☐ Affidavit ☐ Other
DOC DATE J F M A M J   J A S O N D , _____
DOC TITLE or TYPE
OF PAGES _____   ☐ Inspect/Copy Request   Entry X-Ref

SIGNER
☐ SATISFACTORY EVIDENCE ☐ Driver's License / Passport / Other ID **or** ☐ Credible Witness(es) **OR** ☐ Personal Knowledge
SIGNER's NAME
☐ For ☐ Non-Public ADDRESS ☐ Driver's License ☐ Passport ☐ Other ID   ISSUED
PHONE C / H / W   _____ / _____   **or** ☐ MISC   # _____   AGENCY   EXPIRES
SIGNATURE ☐ (oath/affirmation, if any) ☐ (by Mark)

CW #1
#1 WITNESS's NAME
☐ P/Known ADDRESS ☐ Driver's License ☐ Passport ☐ Other ID ISSUED
PHONE C / H / W   _____ / _____   **or** ☐ MISC   # _____   AGENCY   EXPIRES
SIGNATURE ☐ (after oath / affirmation) ❶

CW #2
#2 WITNESS's NAME
☐ P/Known ADDRESS ☐ Driver's License ☐ Passport ☐ Other ID ISSUED
PHONE C / H / W   _____ / _____   **or** ☐ MISC   # _____   AGENCY   EXPIRES
SIGNATURE ☐ (after oath / affirmation) ❷

Entry 100

SERVICE		
DATE _ - _ -20_	TIME _ : _ ☐ am ☐ pm	☐ Stop ☐ Office
MILES	Adv. Travel $	Rush $	Notary $	Copy $	Other $	TOTAL FEES $

NOTES / ADDRESS

Fingerprint
R
T
I
M
R
P
L

TYPE ☐ Acknowledgment ☐ Jurat ☐ Signature Witnessing ☐ Copy Certification ☐ Oath/Affirmation ☐ Protest ☐ Other

DOCUMENT
DOC TYPE ☐ Deed G/QC/W ☐ DOT/Mortgage ☐ Trust Rev/Irrev/Cert ☐ Will ☐ POAF G/L D/S ☐ POAH/AHCD ☐ Affidavit ☐ Other
DOC DATE J F M A M J   J A S O N D , _____
DOC TITLE or TYPE
OF PAGES _____   ☐ Inspect/Copy Request   Entry X-Ref

SIGNER
☐ SATISFACTORY EVIDENCE ☐ Driver's License / Passport / Other ID **or** ☐ Credible Witness(es) **OR** ☐ Personal Knowledge
SIGNER's NAME
☐ For ☐ Non-Public ADDRESS ☐ Driver's License ☐ Passport ☐ Other ID   ISSUED
PHONE C / H / W   _____ / _____   **or** ☐ MISC   # _____   AGENCY   EXPIRES
SIGNATURE ☐ (oath/affirmation, if any) ☐ (by Mark)

CW #1
#1 WITNESS's NAME
☐ P/Known ADDRESS ☐ Driver's License ☐ Passport ☐ Other ID ISSUED
PHONE C / H / W   _____ / _____   **or** ☐ MISC   # _____   AGENCY   EXPIRES
SIGNATURE ☐ (after oath / affirmation) ❶

CW #2
#2 WITNESS's NAME
☐ P/Known ADDRESS ☐ Driver's License ☐ Passport ☐ Other ID ISSUED
PHONE C / H / W   _____ / _____   **or** ☐ MISC   # _____   AGENCY   EXPIRES
SIGNATURE ☐ (after oath / affirmation) ❷

Thank you

for choosing my journal for your notary needs.

Please email questions and suggestions to:

NotaryRecords@gmail.com

... and watch for our companion "Data Shield"

(coming soon)

to help maintain confidentiality of your client data.

Made in the USA
Columbia, SC
06 April 2022

58543184R20041